mountain
bike guide

North York Moors

Villis

www.ernest-press.co.uk

First published by the Ernest Press: 1994
Reprinted with amendments: 1998
© Copyright Sarah and Gary McLeod
New & further enlarged edition: 2010
© Copyright Steve Willis

ISBN 978 0 948153 95 2

British Library Cataloguing-in-publication Data has been
registered with the British Library in Wetherby and is available
on request.

Typeset by Stanningly Serif
Printed by Walker & Connell, Darvel
Bound by Hunter & Foulis, Haddington

Introduction

The Routes

Basemap of Cycle Routes

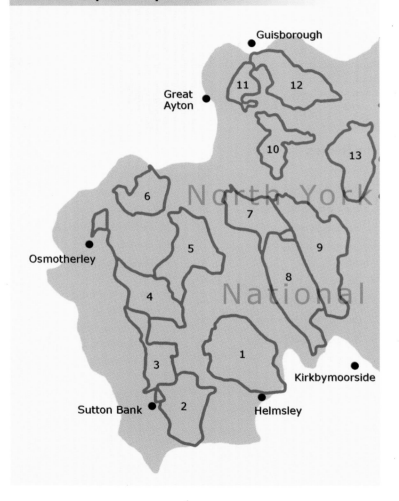

Guisborough

Great Ayton

Osmotherley

North York

National

Kirkbymoorside

Sutton Bank

Helmsley

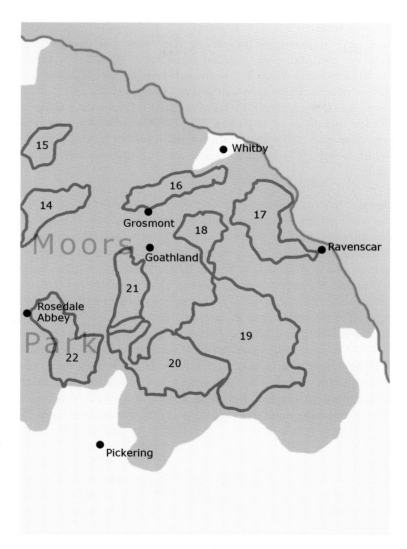

15

14

Whitby

16

Grosmont

18

17

Ravenscar

Goathland

21

Rosedale
Abbey

19

22

20

Pickering

Moors

Park

Publisher's Note

It is always a privilege for me to read and use wonderfully researched mountain bike guidemanuscripts. With Steve Wilis' North York Moors revisions; lush purple heather and wonderfully evocative village names now capture my imagination; as I'm sure 15 years ago Gary & Sarah McLeod original refreshed my father's childhood memories of the place. The North York Moors covers a large area and offers mountain bikers a perfect mix of big sky days out, wonderfully technical trails and undulated scenic valley hopping.

In researching routes and capturing photography for this edition, I was assisted in a fantastic set of circumstances. Groups of unkowns together for a purpose and mixed groups of friends and aquaintences all going for a ride and having a good chat on route. I am indebted to John Dixon for his excellent advice; to Mike Raw and Douglas Roberts (a strong young rider, rightly spotted by GB dev. squad) for their fine company. My sincere thanks also to Mike Hawtin and James Panton of Big Bear Active (Shop and B&B) in Pickering and to John Pitchers of the Appletreewick Bike Livery. All proved to be excellent trail companions and took time out of busy schedules to help. My thanks also to Jon Bateman for his offer of time and to Dave Johnson and Derek Purdy for their superb additional images. I hope this revised guide assists your planning and enjoyment of riding trips in this wonderful area.

Phil Hodgkiss

Introduction to the new edition

Welcome to the 2010 revised edition of our guidebook. There has been a substantial revision of all routes from the 1998 reprint, including two new routes. All photographs are in colour, as are the sketch maps.

The North York Moor National Park

In terms of Landscape, the North York Moors owe their present aspect to the Ice Age, when the effects of glaciations carved out the deep valleys and smoothed off the high moor tops to create the basic topography of the moors. Glacial actions have left exposed or accessible, a wide variety of geological strata which over the centuries has influenced the usage of the moors by its inhabitants: from the earliest Iron Age settlers and the Roman military/civilian immigrants; through the time of harrying by the Norse Invaders; on to the period of expansion by monastic orders. Right through to the time of the Victorian industrialists and their exploitation of the mineral resources of the moors. The area has also witnessed the latest practices of agriculture and industry many of which have left clear reminders of past times in the new predominantly agricultural area. The Moors today still have widely varied uses – from the potage mines on the coast near Loftus, to the moors managed for grouse shooting and sheep grazing – but the industrial usage greatly declined in favour of agriculture and the newest industry, tourism, which is where this guide comes in.

Stunning heather moorland, delightful dales and spectacular coastline with towering cliffs. This begins to give some idea of the amazing and varied geology the North York Moors have to offer. With the largest expanse of moorland heather in the United Kingdom and over 800km of bridleways it's easy to understand why this area is so attractive to mountain bikers and yet compared with relatively well known destinations like the Peak District and Lake District it is still relatively untapped as a UK mountain bikers destination. There are literally hundreds of routes that have something to offer every level of rider with stunning views and great places to stop for a well earned rest along the way. There are easy routes along disused railways, hundreds of miles of twisting singletrack through the heather, fast and flowing drovers road descents, some lung busting climbs and many technical rocky sections that will test the most experienced of riders. As well as the natural and varied terrain of the North York Moors, a visit to the area quite literally offers mountain bikers the best of both worlds. Nestling on the southern edge of the National Park is Dalby Forest, venue for the UCI Cross Country World Cup and home to some of the best forest trails the UK has to offer. From green and blue routes ideal for families to a combined 30 miles of technical red and black routes Dalby really is one of the UK's premier mountain bike trail centres.

Any introduction to the North York Moors wouldn't be complete without also mentioning the Moor to Sea cycle route which links the towns of Pickering, Scarborough and Whitby. The route uses over 80 miles of forest tracks, green lanes, minor roads and dismantled railway. Crossing through forests, moorland, and along the spectacular heritage coastline it takes in some of the most dramatic scenery in North Yorkshire. Whatever your style of riding or level of fitness there are routes to suit and scattered around the Moors and dales landscapes are some beautiful picturesque villages offering places to eat, drink and of course somewhere to stay as a base for exploring this amazing and diverse area of the country.

How to use this guide

The route descriptions, sketch maps and gradient profiles give a feel for the ride in terms of strenuousness, navigation and the technicality of trails involved. The guides are designed for ease of use in planning over a cup of tea at home or referencing from your back pocket/sack while riding. In your armchair or on the trail, the guide book should be used in combination with the relevant OS

map to place your route in the local area. Going off-route in your armchair is irritating but on the trail you could effectively drop off the edge of your earth. In reasonable weather this may not be a problem but in poor conditions, it is potentially dangerous. A start grid reference is provided for each route to help locate starting points. The sketch maps are not necessarily drawn to scale or of comparable scale to each other. We hope the instructions are easy to follow. If instructions do not say otherwise, continue on the track, path, road, line you are on, taking the most obvious well-defined route. If you are unsure how to use grid references, see the margin of any OS Explorer map for explanations of the scale, gradients and icons (Public Rights of Way, General Features etc).

THE COUNTRY CODE

1   Be safe – plan ahead and follow any signs;
2   Leave gates and property as you find them;
3   Protect plants and animals and take your litter
        home;
4   Keep dogs under close control;
5   Consider other people.

OFF ROAD CODE

1   Keep to rights of way – use maps to plan your route
        in advance;
2   Check your bike before you set out;
3   Take adequate supplies of food and drink, water
        proofs, tools and spares;
4   Give way to horses and walkers;
5   Ride in groups of two or three;
6   Be kind to plants and creatures;
7   Prevent erosion;
8   Close gates behind you;
9   Take your litter home and guard against fire.

Public right of way

To make the most of your off-road cycling you need to know where you can or cannot ride. In this section we hope to cover some of the basic terms you may come across to help you plan your own routes.

PUBLIC FOOTPATH – over which there is right of way on foot only. Cyclists have no right of way to ride on a Public Footpath. Footpaths are sometimes waymarked on signs or marker posts by yellow arrows/discs.

BRIDLEWAY – over which there is a public right of way on foot, horseback and pedal cycle, provided that cyclists give way to horse riders and pedestrians. Bridleways are sometimes marked on signs by blue arrows/discs.

BYWAYS/BOATS – open to all traffic

RESTRICTED BYWAY – A highway for use only by walkers, horse riders, cyclists and horsedrawn vehicles but not cars or motorbikes – before 2006 classified as RUPPs. Restricted Byways may be marked by purple waymarks or arrows.

RUPPS – a road used as a public path. Its minimum status was that of a bridleway. However this classification proved unsatisfactory. All RUPPS should have been reclassified as one of the above, though old signs may still exist.

UNCLASSIFIED COUNTY ROAD – a minor road which may not be metalled. It can be regarded as having the same status as a byway. However they are not distinguished from any other road or private track on an OS map.

GREEN LANE – an unsurfaced walled track often of some antiquity. However the term Green Lane has no legal meaning.

TRAILS AND CYCLE TRACKS e.g. often converted old railway lines.

Maps

To supplement the route descriptions or to plan your own rides we reccomend that you use the Ordnance Survey 1:25 000 Explorer maps which cover all of the area in this guide: OL 26 – North York Moors Western Area and OL27 - North York Moors Eastern Area.

Weather

Be prepared for changeable weather on the all routes. The most useful weather forecasts are local on line: Metcheck and BBC.

Allowing Time

The times mentioned at the start of each route are only a rough guide, estimated by riders of medium fitness with average weather and ground conditions. You will learn to judge your own riding speed or that of the slowest rider in your group. Always allow more time than seems necessary so a puncture or long lunch stop doesn't leave you caught out in the dark. Adverse weather (rain, wind, snow and ice) or very wet/soft surfaces can double or triple the time you would normally take to ride an off road stretch. Leave more time for bigger groups.

Clothing

In summer often all you will need are shorts and a tee shirt or short-sleeved cycle top; however maintaining a comfortable body temperature when riding is sometimes difficult. Uphill you can get very hot and sweaty then on the downhills or on exposed ground, quite cold. Most people find wearing a number of layers of the appropriate thickness works best. You can vary the layers, taking them on and off. Usually up to three layers (or more if needed) works well; a base wicking layer, either a short sleeved summer jersey or a soft shell jacket. A waterproof jacket should be carried on all big days out.

Shorts or Trousers – For short journeys you can get away with normal shorts or trousers but on a longer ride or in wet weather, specific cycle shorts with a pad and no uncomfortable seams are much better (lycra or baggies).

Windproof/Waterproofs – Choose a breathable and light-weight waterproof that packs down small, is cut for cycling with a longer back and arms and has reflective piping or patches. Some jackets have pit zips, holes under the arms to help ventilation. I prefer not to wear a waterproof unless it is very cold or raining reasonably hard. They do not breathe as well as a fleece or a wind-shirt so can make you very sweaty and then cold.

Hands and Feet – Keeping hands and feet warm in winter when cycling can be a big problem. They don't move much and are very exposed to wind and water. Buy good gloves, a thin thermal 'buff' or similar (fits under your helmet) and carry them even if you don't think you are going to need them. Don't buy shoes or boots that are tight or wear too many socks as this will restrict the circulation making your feet colder. Cycling specific shoes have a stiff sole that doesn't flex too much. This makes pedalling more efficient and comfortable but make sure you can walk in them. Getting off the bike now and then will help warm feet up, as will making sure your body is warm enough so that it does not restrict blood flow to your extremities.

Helmets – It is good sense to wear a helmet when mountain biking. Modern helmets are light-weight, have adjustable bands to fit the head and are well vented (i.e. cool) so they are comfortable to wear. Always try a helmet for fit before buying it. A peak can help keep sun or rain out of your eyes. Check a helmet has an EU standard (EN1078) or Snell B90/B95. Adjust the strap so the helmet sits squarely on your head protecting your forehead and is not easy to push back.

Food

While riding you consume a high number of calories and lose a lot of water through sweating. Have a good breakfast before you set off. Eat something like a big bowl of oats or cereal for slow release carbohydrates. Always carry some snacks and sandwiches on longer rides, with sugars and carbohydrates that are easily broken down to replace energy. Drink plenty before and during your ride. You can lose litres of water per hour if it is very hot. Adequate fluid intake also helps prevent cramp. Tuck away some extra snacks for emergency rations.

Map, Compass & Whistle

Along with this guide book carry a large-scale map (detailed at the start of each route) and carry a Silva-type compass. This could prove invaluable if you get off course. A whistle is useful for attracting attention and summoning help in emergencies. The international distress signal is six long blasts followed by a minute gap before repeating.

First Aid

A little knowledge of first-aid may well go a long way toward relieving pain, discomfort or even saving a life. A few guidelines or basic instructions and a first-aid kit might just help while stranded out on the hills. First and foremost, it's well worth going on a first-aid course, whether as a first aider at work or as a specialist requirement for outdoor instructing; there will be courses to suit all scenarios. These courses are run by groups such as St Johns Ambulance, the Red Cross or even private companies. If that's not possible or you don't have the time, then follow these basic rules.

General Principles. If required, remove the patient from further injury; ensure the casualty can breathe and that there is no danger to you. Stop any bleeding and make the casualty comfortable. In case of serious injury seek medical help at once by calling the emergency services: remote areas may require the mountain rescue team service.

Animal bites. Wash the affected area thoroughly, pat dry and apply a clean dressing. Seek medical help.

Blisters. Do not pop. Cover the blister with a dry dressing only.

Cuts and grazes. Clean with water and apply a clean sterile dressing, do not apply any ointment or cream.

Insect stings. Remove the sting if visible with sterile tweezers. Do not squeeze or scratch the affected area as this may help spread the poison. Apply a cold compress to relieve pain and swelling. Get medical help if swelling impairs breathing.

Minor wounds. The casualty should sit or lie down. Elevate and support the injured limb if possible if there is no fracture suspected. If there is bleeding apply direct pressure preferably over a clean dressing. Apply a bandage and pad, maintaining pressure. If blood seeps through apply another dressing on top. Do not apply a tourniquet. Seek medical help if bleeding does not stop.

Shock is nearly always present in cases of an accident. The symptoms are: the pulse may feel weak but beating rapidly; the skin will be cold and clammy to touch and a hunger for air. Make the patient comfortable and insulate from the cold.

Exposure is generally caused by exhaustion and a severe chilling of the body surface, usually in wet and windy conditions. This may not be easy to spot while riding in a group but checking for the signs and symptoms should be every member's responsibility: Mental and physical lethargy, Complaints of cold, tiredness and cramp, Lack of understanding of simple instructions, Slurred speech, Irrational or violent behaviour, Abnormality of vision, Collapse and coma, Not all of these symptoms may be present or in the order given. All cases should be treated immediately as the condition can rapidly become serious.

To treat exposure, stop and seek a sheltered area for all the party. Insulate the patient, especially from the ground and prevent any further heat loss. Place the patient in an emergency insulationbag and if possible another member of the party should get in to provide extra body warmth. Talk and encourage the patient to allay anxiety and mental stress. Do not rub the patient to restore circulation. Do not allow any further exertion and do not give alcohol. Seek expert medical help. Prevention is provided by good equipment, prompt action and good leadership but is everyone's duty to safeguard against exposure.

Getting help. If when riding in a group one member has a serious accident and is unable to carry on and requires medical attention the following procedure should be followed. Treat any injuries and make the patient comfortable, keep him warm and treat for shock. If the group is large enough and there is no signal on your mobile phone; two riders should make for the nearest telephone, taking with them a map and the six figure grid reference of the patient, plus as much detail of the injured party as possible. They must also give their own location and stay there until help arrives.

This procedure minimises the risk of getting lost or further injury. Only as a last resort should a member of the party go alone to get help and that person should be a strong rider and proficient map reader. It's worth knowing the international distress signal for any such occasion: Six blasts on a whistle (or shouts or flashes of a torch) followed by a pause of a minute and keep repeating until the signal is heard and a reply of three blasts, shouts or flashes are received. Waving an item of clothing will also help attract attention to you.

Your Bike

Since this guide was first written, mountain bikes have changed considerably. In the mid 1990's most bikes had cro-mo steel frames, cantilever brakes, rigid forks, 21 speed gearing and flat bars. In 2009, mountain bikes are based around either a hard tail or full suspension frame made usually of aluminium and have disc brakes. They predominantly have a long travel fork, 27 speed gearing, wider handlebars and shorter stems. As riding styles have changed and technology advanced, the mountain bike has become more responsive to technical trails and forgiving on the rider. Bike weights vary depending on cost and intended use.

Choosing a bike – Ideally you want a lightish bike that is strong, reliable and has good brakes. Low gear ratios are standard and tyres are readily available for all conditions. You don't need a very expensive bike to enjoy riding off road but a cheaper bike may be heavier and will have a lower specification of gears, wheels, brakes and other componentry. Before buying a bike, Ask advice from friends and your local bike shop. A full suspension bike needs careful set up and is more expensive to run as it will need constant maintenance to work reliably. The benefit is that full suspension is forgiving to the whole body and on a longer days riding; you will be less fatigued or 'beaten up'. A hard tail bike usually weights less and can be more responsive. There is less maintenance required and if you are not riding on really rough or rocky terrain; a hardtail can be more than adequate. Suspension forks do take the 'buzz' out of a trail and are kinder on the wrists, neck and shoulders.

Maintaining your Bike

Get into the routine of washing and oiling your bike regularly. This prolongs the life of gear parts and the chain. By getting into a routine, your bike will become familiar to you. Regular cleaning can also solve problems before they develop; for example, a bent rear derailleur could cause your gears to skip indexing or allow your rear mechanism to go into the spokes. You might see a small crack in the frame or fork or a cut/split in a tyre. Also, you should check your chain regularly for stretch and replace it when required to avoid damaging the cassette and crank rings. You should also check your brake pads for 'life'. Have your bike serviced by a local bike shop or learn to do the maintenance jobs yourself.

Tools & Spares

A sensible tool kit would be: a pump, spare inner tubes, a puncture repair kit, tyre levers and a multi tool that includes all the Allen key sizes required for adjusting your bike. Most multi tools include a chain splitting tool and flat/star headed screwdrivers and a spoke key. On longer or more remote trips you might take zip ties, spare allen bolts, oil & a rag, spare spokes, duct tape, spare brake block/pads and any specific tool that you bike may need, e.g. an air pump for your suspension.

1. Ryedale & Riccaldale

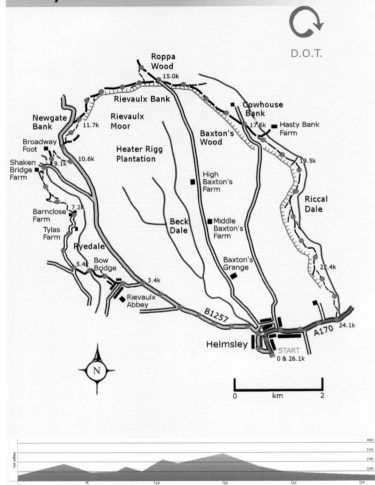

D.O.T.

Roppa Wood
15.0k

Rievaulx Bank

Rievaulx Moor

Newgate Bank
11.7k

Cowhouse Bank
17.6k

Hasty Bank Farm

Baxton's Wood

Broadway Foot

Heater Rigg Plantation

10.6k

Shaken Bridge Farm
9.1k

19.5k

High Baxton's Farm

Riccal Dale

Barnclose Farm
7.2k

Beck Dale

Middle Baxton's Farm

Tylas Farm

Ryedale

Baxton's Grange

5.4k
Bow Bridge

22.4k

3.4k

Rievaulx Abbey

B1257

Helmsley

START
0 & 26.1k

A170 24.1k

N

0   km   2

20

Route Details

Start Grid Ref:
GR 613838 Helmsley market place

Map
OS 26 1:25 000

Distance
Full: 26.1km/16.3m
Short: 18km/11.3m

Height Gain
500m

%age off road
69%

Time
3-4 hours

Facilities
Refreshments at Helmsley

Route Summary

Helmlsey, with NP offices, Castle, shops, cafes and pubs, makes a good place to start & finish. A lovely route at any time of year – spring bluebells in Riccaldale, late summer heather on the moors, autumn colours in Ryedale & somewhere sheltered to ride in winter.

The hard work is done early, with the climb out of Helmsley. From Newgate Bank (at 11km) it's mainly level or downhill. The newly designated bridleway along Reivaulx Bank & Cowhouse Bank, & down Riccaldale must be one of the best additions in the country. Be careful on the B1257 at the start & the A170 as you finish – two very busy roads.

The Route.

Start by leaving the market place on the B1257 towards Stokesley. **TR** then follow the road uphill to the Reivaulx junction (3.4km). **TL** downhill then **R** after 600m on the bend just before the church (the abbey is only 400m further on). Follow this gravel lane for 400m then fork **L** (with a great view of the Abbey over your shoulder) and enjoy the ride down to Bow Bridge where you cross the River Rye before heading up to the track junction (5.4km).

Follow this farm road to Tylas Farm where you **TL** through a gate then down and up to Barnclose Farm (7.2km). **TL** in the farmyard, through the gate then up the grassy track to a bridle post. Bear **R** along a hedge then keep **L** of a gate (don't follow the track into the wood) and climb up the edge of the field to the bridle gate (7.9km). **TR** then bear **L** up the grassy slope towards a barn where you turn sharp **R** down a good track for 50m to a gate.

Through the gate then sharp **L** downhill towards Shaken Bridge Farm. **TR** at the bridle post 100m before the farm, down across the field, through a gate, up to the concrete road then down to the Hawnby road. **TR** over Shaken Bridge (which has been replaced following the flash floods of June 2005) then **L** after 100m and walk up through the woods for 50m – footpath. **TL** along the concrete track to the gate at Broadway Foot. Turn sharp **R** up this excellent single track, sharp **L** then up to a forest road, **L** again for 50m then sharp **R** up the wide forest track to the B1257.

TL for 400m then **R** into Newgate Bank carpark. Bend **L** (it is only a narrow path **SO** through the gate) then straight along a grassy single track as the road bends **R** into the carpark. Below the viewing platform (with excellent views of Easterside Hill and the moors) contour through the trees for 500m before dropping down **L** to the forest road (11.7km). **TR** and follow this vehicle track to the Xrds at Roppa Wood (15km).

SO then **R** at the next track junction and contour along Cowhouse Bank until you reach the tarmac road (17.6km) that you cross before heading down Riccaldale. Keep **R** at the first track junction then follow this good gravel track for 5km always keeping the stream on your **L**. After 22.4km bear **L** along the lesser track (the better one heads up into the woods) until you reach the gate at the end of the woods. Cross the field and you will meet the A170 (24.1km). **TR** and follow this road for 2km back into Helmsley.

Descending the steep, fast & fun singletrack on Reivaulx Bank. Pic: Phil Hodgkiss

Shorter route

As soon as you've left the market place and turned **R** onto the Stokesley road you need to **TR** again just after the church then **L** after 100m in front of the cemetery gates. Follow Baxton's Lane passing the swimming pool and 3 farms until you reach the edge of Reivaulx Bank. After 250m of climbing in 7km you will appreciate the view from the bench before heading down the road to the crossroads in Roppa Wood where you **TR** and follow the main route.

2. Wass Bank & Ryedale

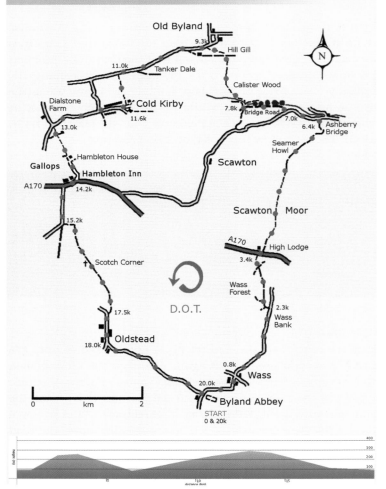

Old Byland
9.3k
Hill Gill
11.0k
Tanker Dale
Calister Wood
Dialstone Farm
Cold Kirby
7.8k
Bridge Road
7.0k
11.6k
6.4k
Ashberry Bridge
13.0k
Seamer Howl
Hambleton House
Scawton
Gallops
Hambleton Inn
A170
14.2k
15.2k
Scawton Moor
A170
High Lodge
Scotch Corner
3.4k
D.O.T.
Wass Forest
2.3k
Wass Bank
17.5k
Oldstead
18.0k
0.8k
Wass
20.0k
Byland Abbey
START
0 & 20k

0   km   2

N

24

Route Details

Start Grid Ref
GR 548790 Byland Abbey Car
Park

Map
OS 26 1:25 000

Distance
20km/12.5m

Height Gain
400m

%age off road
53%

Time
2-3 hours

Facilities
Byland Abbey, Wass, Scawton,
Hambleton, Oldstead

Route Summary

This route takes you through
four beautiful villages and
uses a mixture of forest
tracks, the Cleveland Way,
field edges & minor roads.
Take great care crossing the
busy A170.

The route starts at Byland
Abbey (founded in 1177).
After climbing Wass Bank
cross Scawton Moor. Then
descend towards the River
Rye draining the SW part of
the North York Moors before
climbing back towards Sutton
Bank. The Hambleton Inn is
a welcome refreshment point
before descending past Scotch
Corner Chapel. Although
this building looks ancient
it was built in the 1950s as
a memorial to 3 pupils of
Ampleforth College who died
in the Second World War.

The Route

Start by following the road to Wass (0.8km) and then climb steadily up Wass Bank to the bridleway (2.3km). **TL** then **R** after 50m along forest roads, **SO** at both junctions then along a singletrack to the A170 (3.4km). **TR** carefully along this busy road for 50m then **L** down High Lodge farm track.

The smiling Barn at Ashberry. Pic: Steve Willis

Follow the bridleway signs across the fields through 4 gates until you reach the edge of the woods in Seamer Howl where you follow the vehicle track down to Nettle Dale at Ashberry Bridge (6.4km). **TL** along the road for 600m then **R** along Bridge Road (gravel track) past 5 fishponds. **TR** across the stepping-stones then **R** and **L** along a bridleway that follows a streambed then push up the track through Callister Woods. Bear **R** at the top across 3 fields and the farm road before dropping into Hill Gill, **TL** and follow the edge to the road W of Old Byland (9.3km).

Bear **L** along the road until you reach the bridleway just after Tanker Dale (11km). **TL** along a grassy field edge, down through a gate into a small valley then up and through 3 gates into a farm at Cold Kirby (11.6km). **TR** along the road through the village until you reach the gallops again near Dialstone Farm. **TL** along the edge of the gallops crossing the farm road then down and over an all-weather track. Then through the gate and onto the tarmac road at Hambleton House where you meet the Cleveland Way. Along the road, through the woods and up to the Hambleton Inn (14.2km).

TR along the A170 then **L** towards the White Horse until you reach the first road bend (15.2km). **TL** then bend **R** along a vehicle track through trees to the chapel at Scotch Corner. Continue down this excellent track to the road at Oldstead (17.5km). TL, follow the road through the village bearing **L** at the pub then continue downhill for another 2km back to Byland Abbey (20km).

Shorter Route

When you reach Ashberry Bridge **TL** along Nettle Dale but continue along the road up the hill through Scawton until you reach the A170. **TR** for 600m until you reach the Hambleton Inn then follow the main route.

Byland abbey. Pic: Steve Wills

3. The Hambleton Hills

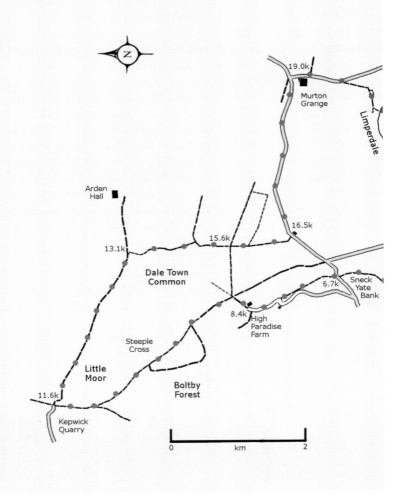

19.0k
Murton
Grange

Limperdale

Arden
Hall

16.5k

13.1k

15.6k

Dale Town
Common

Sneck
Yate
Bank

6.7k

8.4k High
Paradise
Farm

Steeple
Cross

Little
Moor

Boltby
Forest

11.6k

Kepwick
Quarry

0   km   2

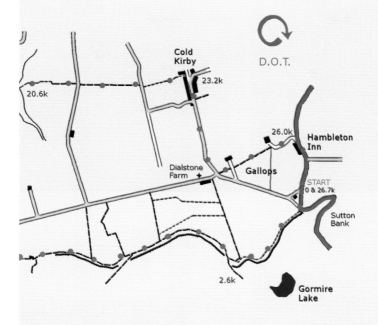

Cold Kirby

23.2k

20.6k

D.O.T.

26.0k

Hambleton Inn

Dialstone Farm

Gallops

START
0 & 26.7k

Sutton Bank

2.6k

Gormire Lake

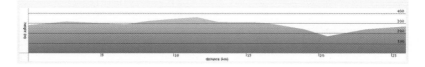

Gormie Lake from Sutton Bank. Pic: Steve Willis

Looking towards Hawnby Hill. Pic: Steve Willis

Route Details

Start Grid Ref
GR 516831 Sutton Bank
Visitor Centre

Map
OS 26 1:25 000

Distance
Full: 26.7km/16.4m
Short: 20km/12.5m

Height gain
200m

%age off road
75%

Time
2-3 hours

Facilities:
Sutton Bank Visitor Centre
and the Hambleton Inn

Route Summary

This route follows the top of the Whitestone Cliff from Gormire Lake (one of only four natural lakes in the county) to Sneck Yate. It offers tremendous views over the northern Vale of York and across to the Dales.

Please take care along the cliff top track, as it is very busy at weekends and muddy when wet. Then it is a mixture of forestry, moorland and rolling farmland on the dip slope east of the escarpment with superb views of the Moors

The Route

From the carpark, take the minor road **NE** across the gallops towards the mast at Dialstone Farm. **TL** at the road junction then **L** again immediately in front of the farm along a good track. Follow the bridleway **SW** for 800m until you reach the wall protecting the top of Whitestone Cliff. Bear **R** until you come to the signpost where you **TR** along the cliff top path (2.6km). Take a moment to walk 20m to the left for a superb view over Gormire Lake.

Keep the cliff on your left as you follow this superb track for 2.5km past several bridleways, quarries and a (very ruined) Roman signal station until you arrive at the Sneck Yate Road (6.7km). Cross the road into Boltby Forest along a single track to the road bend at Low Paradise then bear **R** up the road to High Paradise (8.4km).

Short Route: go across Dale Town Common after High Paradise.

Keep **L** of the farm along a track to the Hambleton (Drovers) Road where you **TL** until you reach the forest again. Pass along the eastern edge of the woods to Steeple Cross (just a small standing stone now) where you head out across the moors for 2.5km with superb views towards Black Hambleton.

At the road/bridleway junction with 'no access' signs (11.6km) turn sharply **R** on a good track for 2.5km across Arden Moor through 2 gates. 350m after the second gate just at the start of a steep downhill section **TR** up a good track. Head **S** across the field towards a single tree then down into a shallow valley with a gate.

Through the gate and up onto the moor keeping the wall on your **L** for 1.5km passing a small wood and crossing another shallow valley to the bridleway junction (15.6km). **SO** through the gate and keep heading south to the copse and (ruined) Silver Hill Farm 16.5km). **TL** along the road through the woods at the Peak Scar climbing area to another road junction above Hawnby (19km). Definitely a camera moment.

TR along the road past Murton Grange then go **SO** where the road bears **L** just after a dip onto a good track across a field. Bear **R** down into Limperdale and carefully follow the bridleway signs eventually dropping **L** through a gate and down to the streams (20.6km). Over both bridges then walk up the steep path (passing a handy bench half way up) onto the plateau and follow the field edge **S** to the road.

TR then **L** after 20m along a good track down into a dry valley then up beside a wall to the next road. Again **TR** then **L** after 20m along a grassy field edge, down through a gate into a small valley then up and through 3 gates into a farm at Cold Kirby (23.2km).

TR along the road through the village until you reach the gallops again near Dialstone Farm. **TL** along the edge of the gallops crossing the farm road then down and over an all weather track. Give way to any horses then through the gate and onto the tarmac road at Hambleton House where you meet the Cleveland Way. Along the road through the woods and up to the Hambleton Inn (26km). **TR** along the A170 for 700m back to the visitors centre.

4. Hambleton Road and Ryedale

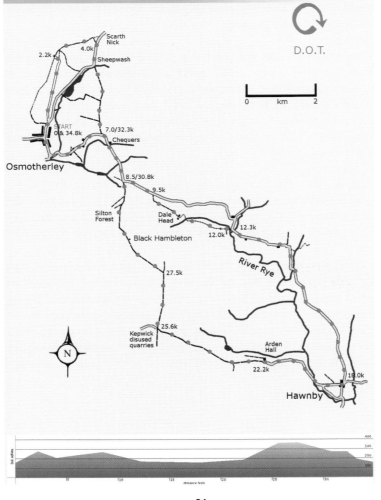

D.O.T.

Scarth Nick
4.0k
2.2k
Sheepwash

0   km   2

START
0 & 34.8k   7.0/32.3k
Chequers
Osmotherley

8.5/30.8k
9.5k

Silton
Forest
Dale
Head
12.0k   12.3k
Black Hambleton

River Rye

27.5k

25.6k
Kepwick
disused
quarries
Arden
Hall
22.2k
18.0k

N

Hawnby

Route 4: Hambleton Road & Ryedale

Route Details

Start Grid Ref
GR 457972 Osmotherley

Map
OS26 1:25 000

Distance
Full: 34.8km/22m
Short: 25km/15.6m

Height Gain
700m

%age off road
57%

Time
3-4 hours

Facilities
Osmotherley, Chequers,
Hawnby Hotel

Route Summary

This route takes in some gentler landscape along the western edge of the Moors. It also has a handily located Hawnby Hotel about halfway along the route. The ascent afterwards is along a well surfaced track; the old drovers' road towards Black Hambleton.

It's a pleasure to ride, with a long downhill back to the road leading to Chequers. At times, you will be following the route of the Hambleton Drove Road that, at its peak in the early 19th century saw 100,000 cattle per year heading from Scotland.

The route

Starting from the market cross in Osmotherley, head **N** up the road to the speed limit sign then bear **L** up the tarmac bridleway towards the booster station. As this road bends **L** after 2.2km go **SO** through the left hand gate along a good track to meet the Cleveland Way. Through the gate then down a lovely track to the spur where you bend **R** down to the road at Scarth Nick (4km). **TR** and follow the road to Sheepwash where you ford the river as the road bends **R** before pushing up the old drovers' road

for 100m then continuing south along this excellent track to meet the road (7km) just north of Chequers.

Continue **S**, **TL** at the sharp bend (8.5km) then **R** after 1km onto a good track through the heather down to a gate. Bear **L** then down to Dale Head (ruin). Down through the fields across a bridge then a short push up before a lovely singletrack across the moor to a gate (12km). Follow the edge of the field to another gate then **TL** on a farm track that bends down to a bridge and the road at Wheat Beck (12.3km). Uphill from the bend past Lane House Farm where the road bends sharp **R**, then down and round the hairpin bends in Ellers Wood.

Past the picnic area with superb views down Ryedale before a gentle climb to the south end of Hawnby Hill before a fast descent into

Vivid heather and fantastic wilderness trails. Moorland pleasures. Pic Steve Wills

the village of Hawnby (18km). Bend **R** then **SO** past the Hawnby Hotel towards Arden Hall (22.2km). The tarmac road ends here and, ignoring the bridleway sign pointing towards the hall, head uphill on an excellent track through the woods until you come out onto the open moor. The gradient lessens and you eventually reach the Cleveland Way at thecrossroads (25.6km) above the disused Kepwick quarries. **TR** towards White Gill Head where you turn sharp **L** (27.5km) and climb along the western flank of Black Hambleton. Just after the cairn above Silton Woods there is an excellent descent down to the road bend (30.8km).

Follow the road past Chequers again and bear **R** along the track as the road bends **L** (32.3km). Follow this excellent track again for 1km before turning **L** at the Route 65 sign, down through the woods then **L** and **R** before reaching the dam at Cod Beck Reservoir (33.3km). Cross the dam, up the track to meet the road then **TL** down to Osmotherley (34.8km).

Short Route
Start and finish at Chequers and leave Cod Beck Reservoir for another day.

5. Bilsdale

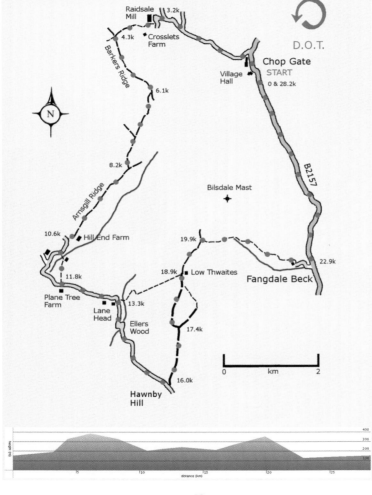

Raidsale Mill
3.2k
4.3k
Crosslets Farm
Barker's Ridge
6.1k
8.2k
Arnsgill Ridge
10.6k
Hill End Farm
11.8k
Plane Tree Farm
Lane Head
13.3k
Ellers Wood
16.0k
Hawnby Hill
17.4k
18.9k
Low Thwaites
19.9k
Bilsdale Mast
22.9k
Fangdale Beck
B2157
Chop Gate
START
0 & 28.2k
Village Hall
D.O.T.
N

0   km   2

400
300
200
100

altitude (m)

5   10   15   20   25
distance (km)

Route Details

Start Grid Ref
GR 558994 Chop Gate Village
Hall car park

Map
OS 26 1:25 000

Distance
28.2km/17.6m

Height Gain
450m

%age off road
54%

Time
3-4 hours

Facilities
Buck Inn at Chop Gate

Route Summary

Very open moorland terrain above Bilsdale where you will be aware of the peaceful space that the moors have to offer. Not much shelter in poor weather but two superb downhill sections make the route worthwhile in all seasons.

Navigation should be fairly straight forward – just take care when you turn right off the moor and head down into Bildale or you will end up on the wrong (south) side of Fangdale Beck.

The Route

TL out of the carpark, passing the Buck Inn before turning **L** along the road towards Carlton in Cleveland. Follow this road **NW** to Raisdale Mill where you **TL** (3.2km). Down between the buildings then **R** at the marker arrows up Mill Lane. You will need to push most of the 600m up this sunken green lane but it is worth it when you reach the open moorland.

Cross a good track and continue up beside the wall until you reach the track that comes from Crossletts Farm. **SO** at the 'Green Lane' sign and follow this good track which bears **L** towards the overhead wires on the ridge above (4.5km).

TL at the track junction along Barkers Ridge then through a gate, continue **S** towards Bilsdale mast until you meet a track forking **L** at the highest point (6.1km). Bear **R** here then head **SW** down a superb track until you reach the T-junction above Arnsgill, 400m **SW** of a wood (8.2km).

TR down Arnsgill Ridge until you leave the moor at a gate (10km) just after another wood. Continue downhill through the fields on a good track to Hill End Farm where your **TR** then **L** to the road junction (10.6km). **TL** down the concrete road, over a ford then **L** after 150m and over a new footbridge.

SO over a rough field to a groove at the bottom of the woods then straight up through the woods and across a field to a gate in front of a building. **TR** through another gate then contour along a track through 4 fields to meet the road at Plane Tree Farm (11.8km). **TL** and follow the road past Lane House (13.3k), down through Ellers Wood then across the moor to the col **N** of Hawnby Hill (16km). Turn sharp **L** just before the cattle

The Buck Inn at Chop Gate. Pic: Steve Willis

grid along an excellent track towards the mast and trees on the skyline. Ignore the bridleway after 1.4km and continue to the ruin at Low Thwaites (18.9km). Keep **L** of the wall for 1km until you reach the **NW** corner (19.9km) where you **TR** for 200m to the **NE** corner. Bear **L** across the moor at a metal stake and small cairn and follow the single track **ENE** past 4 boundary stones before dropping down to cross the upper part of Fangdale Beck.

Head for a groove through the heather on the far side of the stream then bear **R** at a cairn keeping the beck on your **R** until you start to descend through bracken, over a ruined wall then steeply down a rocky groove to a gate.

Down through the fields then **R** and **L** into the village of Fangdale

Beck. Through a garden onto the road until you reach the main road (B1257) at the green telephone box (22.9km). This road can be busy at weekends So take care while enjoying the superb scenery of Bilsdale on either side as you **TL** and ride 5km back to the village hall.

Shorter route (This is not an easy option as it mainly a push through the heather). **TL** off the road at the bridleway sign just after Lane House. Straight down the first field then diagonally down to Blow Gill that you will have to wade.. Diagonally **L** up the hill until you nearly reach the wall then bear **R** through the heather until you see some trees ahead on the sky line. Head for the right hand ones which are just in front of Low Thwaites where you will **TL** along the full route.

[Rte 7] Frequently winter days can provide some excellent riding, but there are limits. On this occasion even the civilised Rutland Rigg was out of bounds. Pic: Derek Purdy

6. Carlton Bank & Scugdale

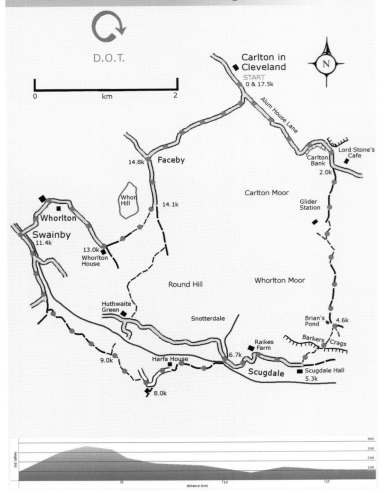

D.O.T.

0   km   2

Carlton in
Cleveland
START
0 & 17.5k

N

Alum House Lane

14.8k   Faceby

Lord Stone's
Cafe

Carlton
Bank
2.0k

Whorl
Hill

14.1k

Carlton Moor

Glider
Station

Whorlton
Swainby
11.4k

13.0k
Whorlton
House

Round Hill

Whorlton Moor

Huthwaite
Green

Snotterdale

Brian's
Pond   4.6k

Barkers Crags

9.0k

Harfa House

6.7k

Raikes
Farm

Scugdale   Scugdale Hall
5.3k

8.0k

altitude (m)

400
300
200
100

|5 |10 |15

distance (km)

Route 6: Carlton Bank & Scugdale

Route Details

Start Grid Ref
GR 508044 Carlton in
Cleveland

Map
OS 26 1:25 000

Distance
17.3km/11m

Height Gain
340m

%age off road
59%

Time
2-3 hours

Facilities
Carlton, Lord Stones, Swainby
and Faceby

Route Summary

This is a quiet ride once
you leave the Carlton Bank
road – the hardest climb on
the route. The area where
the Cleveland Way crosses
your route is popular with
hangliders and, on a bright,
breezy weekend, the air seems
full of them, added to by the
presence of the gliding club
further up the hillside.

There are also clues to the
industrial heritage of the area
with various spoilheaps on
the hillsides – particularly the
old alum quarries on Carlton
Bank.

The Route

Head **SE** out of the village towards Chop Gate along Alum House Lane. The lane soon starts to climb towards Carlton Bank, over a cattle grid then **L** with the reclaimed alum quarries on your right. At the top of the bank (2km) bear **R** (as the road bends **L** towards Lord Stones cafe) through 2 gates and along a good track towards the glider station.

After 900m take the singletrack bridleway bearing **L** as the track bears **R** at an access sign. Follow the bridleway signs through the heather heading mainly south until you start to descend on a good track to Brian's Pond (4.6km). **TR** at the signpost (ignoring the footpath and private track ahead) through the heather for 200m to the top of Barkers Crags. Carefully look down and you will see the gate you need 100m below.

It is probably best to bear **L** before you go down the end of the crags. After the gate it is a technical descent down to Scugdale Hall (5.3km). **TR** on the road passing Raikes Farm on the hairpin bend then take the farm track (byway) on your **L** as you cross a small stream (6.7km). Follow this rough track for 1km to Harfa House then continue along the better track to Harfa Bank Farm (8km).

TR down the tarmac road and take the bridleway on your **L** immediately after the covered reservoir. Down a good track then bear **R** across 5 fields (with gates) until you meet the Cleveland Way (9km). Through the final gate and down this excellent, popular track to the corner of the wood, **L** then immediately R, through a gate and down to the road which takes you into Swainby (11.4km).

TR over the bridge next to the church and follow the road past a ruined castle and church where you bend **R** into Whorlton. Continue on this road to Whorlton House (13kms) where you **TL** along a farm track then across 3 fields and down to the road at Faceby (14.1km). **TL** to the crossroads at the Sutton Arms where you **TR** (14.8km) and head back to Carlton (17.5km)

Shorter route

While heading down Scugdale do not **TL** towards Harfa House but continue along the road to the telephone box at Huthwaite Green. **TR** along the Cleveland Way for 600m until you reach the bottom of the steep steps. Do not go up the steps but go **SO** through a gate and follow the edge of the woods to a (muddy) gate, into the woods and up a good track then **TL** along another excellent singletrack for 600m until you reach another gate.

Out of the woods and diagonally down across a field. Through the gate and **TL** along a good track until you reach Faceby, then as above.

[Rte 7]The un-snowbownd Rutland Rigg - riding with the wonderful big sky feeling.
Pic: Steve Willis

7. Clay Bank & Bransdale

D.O.T.

Clay Bank Car Park

START
0 & 24.0k
B1257
22.9k
1.1k
Carr Ridge
21.8k
Round Hill
Urra Moor
3.2k
5.1k
Bloworth Crossing
5.7k
20.2k
Bilsdale
Bransdale Moor
Rudland Rigg
Tripsdale
18.2k
17.2k
16.0k
Nab End Moor
Cockayne
9.1k
7.8k
Stump Cross
14.5k
10.5k
Breck House
Bransdale
0   km   2
12.5k

50

Route 7: Clay Bank & Bransdale

Route Details

Start Grid Ref
GR 573035 Clay Bank
car park on B1257

Map
OS 26 1:25 000

Distance
24km/15m

Height Gain
560m

%age off road
83%

Time
3 - 4 hours

Facilities
None available (but snack
van in carpark on summer
weekends)

Route Summary

This is a very demanding
route that starts with a walk
up the cobbled bridleway
onto Carr Ridge. However, it
is worth it as the moorland
scenery is brilliant and
the rest of the riding is
varied and interesting. The
Cleveland Way can be busy at
weekends and you pass the
highest point on the moors
(451m) at Round Hill.

Navigation is straightforward
but don't ride too fast down
Rudland Rigg or you will
miss the track down into
Bransdale. The mapped
bridleway west of Tripsdale
doesn't exist so follow the
estate tracks as described in
the route.

The Route

TL out of the carpark heading **S** along the B1257 for 300m before turning **L** up the Cleveland Way. You will need to push your bike up most of this cobbled section until you reach the second gate on the end of Carr Ridge (1.1km). Follow the L-hand track up the ridge bearing **L** then past the cairn on Round Hill (3.4km) before descending down Cockayne Head. Go **SO** when the track bends **L** onto a short single track before turning **R** on the old railway track to Bloworth Crossing (5.7km).

TR down Rudland Rigg passing 2 tracks on your **R**, a footpath on your **L** to the junction (7.8km) where you **TR** across the moor on a quad track. This deteriorates as you descend and bear **L** towards the wood before becoming grassy after the wood corner across the fields down to the road in Bransdale (9.1km).

TR and ride around the dale head with pleasant views in every direction. Ignore the road towards Breck House and climb up the dale road (ignoring the first bridleway) until the road levels out on the open moor (12.5km). Turn sharp **R** along an excellent track heading **N** to Stump Cross (14.5km) where you bear **L**. Continue past 2 shooting huts (16km) before dropping down the hairpin bends into Tripsdale (17.2km). Cross the bridge then up the new track on to Nab End Moor (18.2km).

TR in front of the wall corner then follow the vehicle track **N** along the escarpment with superb views down into Bilsdale. **TL** at the junction (20.2km) down a technical single track then bear **R** at a small cairn (just before the track drops steeply down an ancient gully to a gate) and head across the moor towards the wall. This singletrack is boggy but has been improved and contours around Urra Moor before crossing the stream (21.8km). Don't be tempted to negotiate the awkward rocky steps but follow the level track to the **R** that crosses the stream above a small waterfall. Bear **L** and climb gradually back onto Carr Ridge before going through the gate and back down the Cleveland Way. Please keep to the cobbled track even if the grass looks tempting – even the most technical riders will have to walk down the steepest section by the end of the earthworks. **TR** at the road back to the carpark (24km).

Approaching Bloworth Crossing. Pic: Derek Purdy

8. Bransdale

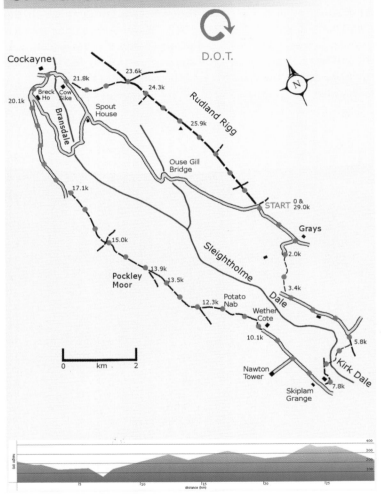

D.O.T.

Cockayne

21.8k

23.6k

24.3k

Rudland Rigg

20.1k

Breck Ho

Cow Sike

Bransdale

Spout House

25.9k

Ouse Gill Bridge

17.1k

START   0 & 29.0k

Grays

Sleightholme Dale

2.0k

15.0k

13.9k

13.5k

Pockley Moor

3.4k

12.3k   Potato Nab

Wether Cote

5.8k

10.1k

Kirk Dale

0   km   2

Nawton Tower

7.8k

Skiplam Grange

Route Details

Start Grid Ref
GR659927 RudlandRigg/
Bransdale Road junction

Map
OS26 1:25 000

Distance
Full: 29km/18m
Short: 18km/11.3m

Height Gain
560m

%age off road
65%

Time
3 - 4 hours

Facilities
The Plough in Fadmoor

Route Summary

This route visits the little known Sleightholmdale and Kirkdale before climbing onto Pockley Moor and following the old byway. It is improving after being badly eroded but still awkward to ride in wet conditions.

You then drop into Bransdale passing the hamlet and church of Cockayne before climbing up an excellent track onto Rudland Rigg where the Moors open out in front of you and the descent back to the start is exhilarating.

The Route

Head **S** down the road to Grays (1.4km), turn sharp **R** along the tarmac lane for 600m onto the bridleway on the second bend. Down the track, through a gate into a field and follow the hedge to another gate at the edge of a wood. Follow the track along the top of this wood through 2 more gates where you reach the road in Sleightholmedale (3.4km).

TL for 1600m (ignoring the footpath to Hold Caldron) until the road bends sharp **L** where you bear **R** for 250m to the signpost (5.8km). **TR** down through the woods to the gate in the valley where you bear **L** for 100m then **TR** across the fields to the stream in Kirk Dale.

Across the bridge then bear **L** up the hill to meet the forest road, **TL** up the hill to the gate. Across the fields to Skiplam Grange, through the gate then **L** to the road (7.8km). **TR** passing Nawton Towers until you reach Wether Cote where the tarmac finishes (10.1km).

SO along the byway (which is marked incorrectly on the 2007 map) and follow the edge of Aldergate Bank with superb views all the way, past Potato Nab until you reach the junction just after the trig point (12.3km). Bear **R** down the good track then across fields to Pockley Moor (13.5km). Through the gate to the muddy junction (13.9km) then be patient on the over-used track across the moor until you reach a track junction by a new gravel pit (15km).

SO for another 2km until you reach the road (17.1km) where you bear **R** for 1km before dropping down into Bransdale. There is a bridleway across the valley and (Short Route by heading straight into Bransdale) but you will have to negotiate 10 gates in 1km.

I prefer to follow the road round the head of the valley below St Nicholas Church at Cockayne (21km) before climbing up the road to the bridleway junction at Cow Sike (21.8km). **TL** up an excellent track onto Rudland Rigg (23.6km) where you **TR** along this well used byway across the moors before descending back to the road junction (29km).

Looking down into Bransdale. Pic: Steve Willis

9. Farndale

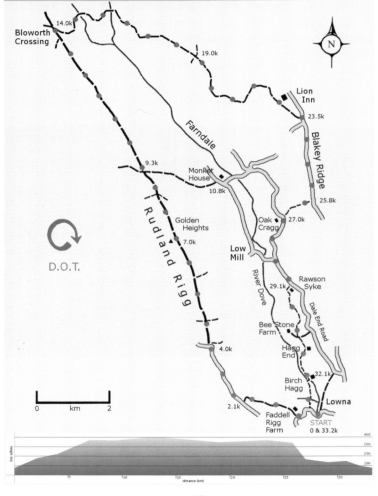

Bloworth Crossing

14.0k

19.0k

Lion Inn

23.5k

Blakey Ridge

Farndale

9.3k

Monket House

10.8k

25.8k

Oak Cragg

27.0k

Golden Heights

7.0k

Low Mill

Rudland Rigg

D.O.T.

River Dove

Rawson Syke

29.1k

Dale End Road

Bee Stone Farm

Hagg End

4.0k

Birch Hagg

32.1k

0   km   2

2.1k

Lowna

Faddell Rigg Farm

START
0 & 33.2k

distance (km)

Route 9: Farndale

Route Details

Start Grid Ref
GR 68591 Lowna car park (1 mile north of Gillamoor)

Map
OS 26 1:25 000

Distance
33.2km/20.7m

Height Gain
350m

%age off road
80%

Time
4-5 hours

Facilities
Lion Inn on Blakey Rigg and Royal Oak at Gillamoor

Route Summary

Most of the hard work is done on the first half of the map on this route and the old railway line from Bloworth Crossing to Blakey Rigg is worth the climb.

The route down Farndale is very scenic and takes you over the River Dove – haunt of coach loads of tourists in the spring when the famous Farndale daffodils are in flower along the riverbanks.

The Route

From the carpark **TR** onto the road, ignore the road to Farndale and continue for 300m to the track to Faddell Rigg Farm. **TR**, go up through the farmyard then along a good track through the fields, **SO** at a bridleway junction in the corner of a wood then sharp **L** up a field edge to the road (2.1km). **TR** and climb to the end of the Rudland Rigg byway (4.0km). Go **SO** (as the road bends **L**) and climb steadily along this excellent tracks passing the trig point (7.0km) on Golden Heights to the bridleway junction (which links Bransdale with Farndale).

SO for another 5 km until you reach Bloworth Crossing and most of the climbing is done. (14km). **TR** and follow this excellent old ironstone railway line for 9km as it contours above Farndale to the Lion Inn on Blakey Rigg. (If you need refreshments you will have to leave the route and follow a track across the moor for 200m past a field barn). When you reach the road (23.5km), **TL** then **R** and head south along Blakey Rigg to the bridleway signpost (25.8km). **TR** and head across the moor towards the fields.

There is no track but head for the wall corner in the distance making sure you keep **R** of the stream source before dropping down an old gully to the bridle gate. Down through the gate then follow the good track around the edge of newly planted trees before dropping down to the road at Oak Cragg (27km). **TL** and **SO** at the road junction and continue for 800m to Rawson Syke where you **TR** down the old byway. This is a tough little section but worth riding if it is dry as it gradually descends down to the River Dove.

After crossing the track to Bee Stone Farm (30.8km) you cross a stream then **TL** through a gate (and don't follow the better track which is only a public footpath heading for Dale End Bridge)

Sometimes the sunset is a perfect end to a ride. Pic: Derek Purdy

crossing 3 fields before you arrive at Hagg End Farm. Through 2 gates and another 2 fields before entering Birch Hagg Plantation. Follow the obvious track gradually down to the house where you cross the garden then **TR** over the bridge. Follow the W side of the river for 800m until you reach a small stream where you bend **R** then **L** over the ford and up the track back to the carpark.

Shorter routes

17km Follow the main route for 9.3km to the bridleway junction on Rudland Rigg. **TR** down the good track towards Monket House taking care on the steepest and more eroded section down to the fields. When you reach the road (10.8km) **TR** and enjoy the ride down to Low Mill where you **TL**, down over the River Dove then up to the T-junction (12km). **TR** for 800m until you reach Rawson Syke then follow the main route

Wet day option

The old byway from Rawson Syke to Lowna is tough riding if it is wet so you may prefer to stay on Dale End road as it gradually climbs out of Farndale. 300m before you reach the Blakey Rigg road **TR** down a large (but sometimes loose) byway to Lowna Bridge where you **TR** and follow the road back to the carpark.

The gate above Oak Cragg. Pic: Steve Willis

10. Baysdale

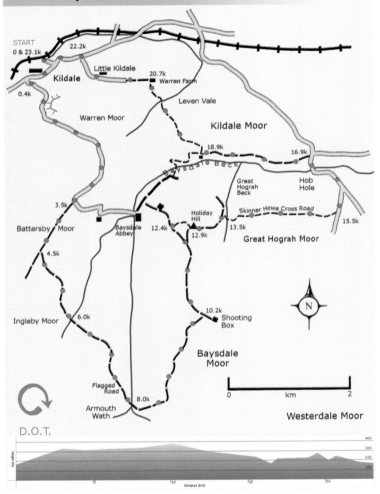

START
0 & 23.1k
22.2k
Kildale
Little Kildale
20.7k
Warren Farm
0.4k
Leven Vale
Warren Moor
Kildale Moor
18.9k
16.9k
Baysdale Beck
Great
Hograh
Beck
Hob
Hole
3.5k
Holiday
Hill
Skinner Howe Cross Road
15.5k
Battersby Moor
Baysdale
Abbey
12.4k
13.5k
12.9k
Great Hograh Moor
4.5k
Ingleby Moor
6.0k
10.2k
Shooting
Box
N
Baysdale
Moor
Flagged
Road
8.0k
0   km   2
Armouth
Wath
Westerdale Moor

D.O.T.

Route Details

Start Grid Ref
GR 605095 Kildale Station

Map
OS 26 1:25 000

Distance
Full: 23.1km/14.4m
Short: 20, 16 or 13km
         12.5, 10 or 7.8m

Height Gain
440m

%age off road
74%

Time
3-4 hours

Facilities
Kildale village shop

Route Summary

This route is physically demanding and you traverse some very unused moorland so make sure your equipment is in good order before you set off. Armouth Wath is as remote as anywhere in the Moors but the estate tracks over Baysdale Moor have improved in recent years.

The views are spectacular, the Skinner Howe Cross Road is not a road but a technical section of singletrack and the final climb onto Kildale Moor will test your fitness

The Route

From the station ride up to the village, **TR** past the village shop for 400m then **TL** along the road that follows the Cleveland Way. This climbs onto Warren Moor becoming more gradual until it turns sharp left (3.5km) where you go **SO** across Battersby Moor. After 1km.

TL over Ingleby Moor. There is a short climb after crossing a small beck then follow the Flagged Road (which isn't flagged) before dropping down to the ruin at Armouth Wath (8.3km). A 50m push up the vehicle track brings you onto Baysdale Moor with superb views down into Westerdale and follow the good track to the junction above the shooting box (10.5km).

TL then bear **L** down to the woods above Baysdale Abbey (12.4km). **TR** along the single track by the fence for 100m before turning **R** up to a cairn on Holiday Hill where you rejoin a vehicle track (12.9km). Bear **L** for 300m to the junction then **TL** for 100m before turning sharp **R** diagonally down to the old bridge over Great Hograh Beck (13.5km).

Push up the single track towards a cairn on Great Hograh Moor then follow the technical single track (called Skinner Howe Cross Road) for 2km to the road (15.5km). **TL** then **L** again down to the ford at Hob Hole before climbing to the junction (16.9km).

TL along a good track above Baysdale Beck to the bridleway junction at an old building (18.9km), where you **TR** and push up to a cairn on Kildale Moor. Through a gate then bear **R** and down a difficult section of moorland before descending along 2 field edges while heading towards a large chimney in Leven Vale (20.3km). Cross the stream before bearing **L** then **R** up the field to Warren

Crossing the ford at Hob Hole. Riders John Dixon & Douglas Robertson. Pic: Phil Hodgkiss

Farm. Through the gate then **L** and down the track which soon becomes tarmac, through Little Kildale before reaching the main road (22.2km). **TL** for 400m into Kildale then **R** and back to the station.

Shorter routes

20km

Follow the main route for 12.4km to the woods above Baysdale Abbey where you go through the gate and down to Thorntree House. Through the gate then down to the main track where you **TR** for 700m to the barn at the track bend. Bear **L** through a gate and over the stream before climbing up through the fields to the moor below a large cairn on the skyline. **TR** along a wet bridleway for 600m to an old building then **TL** to follow the main route (16km) or go **SO** to follow the short route (20km).

13km

Follow the main route for 3.8km to the sharp road bend on Battersby Moor where you stay on the road and descend to Baysdale Abbey. Bear **L** and cross Baysdale Beck on a good track for 800m then bear **L** down to the stream just where the track bends right at a barn. Cross the stream then push up the fields to the moor below a large cairn on the skyline. **TR** along a wet bridleway for 600m to an old building then continue **E** along a good track to the road junction. **TL** and climb over Kildale Moor, down and over the railway line, up through Crag Bank Wood then **L** back to Kildale.

[Rte 11]. Pasing below Captan Cook's Monumanet. Riders Douglas Roberts & John Dixon. Pic: Phil Hodgkiss

11. Captain Cook's Tour

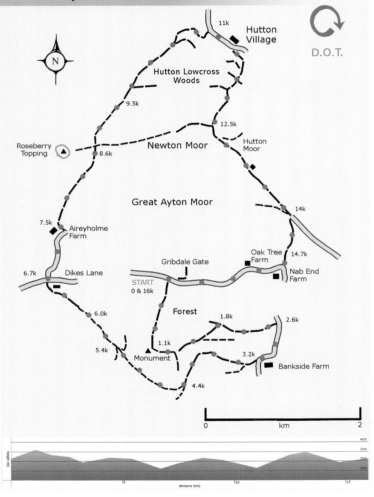

D.O.T.

11k
Hutton Village

Hutton Lowcross Woods

9.5k

12.5k

Roseberry Topping

8.6k

Newton Moor

Hutton Moor

Great Ayton Moor

14k

7.5k
Aireyholme Farm

14.7k
Oak Tree Farm

Gribdale Gate

Nab End Farm

6.7k
Dikes Lane

START
0 & 16k

6.0k

Forest

1.8k

2.6k

1.1k

3.2k

5.4k
Monument

Bankside Farm

4.4k

0   km   2

Route Details

Grid Ref
GR 593110 Gribdale Gate
car park (1 mile east of Great
Ayton Station)

Map
OS26 1:25 000

Distance
16km/10m

%age off road
81%

Height Gain
500m

Time
2½ - 3½ hours

Facilities
Great Ayton or refreshment
van in carpark in summer

Route Summary

This is a shorter ride that offers a good mix of terrain, superb views and fairly simple navigation. The area around the start is popular with the local mountain bike riders so you might find the first climb up to Captain Cook's Monument harder than normal.

As well as the monument (erected in 1827) you will also pass Aireyholme Farm where the young James Cook spent much of his childhood. Roseberry Topping dominates many of the views – its peculiar shape is due to a geological fault and a mining collapse early in the 20th-century.

The Route

Head **S** up the hill through the forest to Captain Cook's Monument (1.1km) then **TL** across the moor and back into the forest. After 400m leave the Cleveland Way by bearing **L** along a good track to the forest road where you **TR** and follow to the road (2.6km).

TR and down the hill to Bankside Farm where you bear **R** to the forest gate on the sharp **L** bend (3.2km). Follow this lovely track through the woods for 1200m before bearing **R** at the signpost along a single track, through a gate then beside a wall below the monument on the moor above until you reach the trees (5.4km).

Through a gate, across a track, through 2 more gates then bear **L** to a wall corner and down to a gate (6km). Down a technical section over some awkward roots then along a good track to Dikes Lane (6.7km). Straight across then follow Aireyholme Lane to the farm (7.5km).

Captain Cook's Monument. Pic: Steve Willis

TL then **R** along a good track between hedges heading towards Roseberry Topping until you reach the col (8.6km). Through the gate, slightly **L** across the common before descending to a gate then head for the forest (9.5km). Follow the main track as it improves in Hutton Lowcross Woods (which has an excellent network of mountain bike routes) and gradually descend to the edge of the forest above the village (10.7km).

Through the gate then stay on the main track which curves round to the road (11k). **TR** into Hutton Village, taking the first bridleway on your **R** after 300m signposted Kildale and Commondale. Climb this good gravel track through the woods passing one large junction until you reach Hutton Moor (12.5km). Through 2 gates then follow the good track uphill ignoring the Cleveland Way on your **L** and an indistinct bridleway on your **L**.

TR to reach a brick ruin (13.3km) before heading down to the road end(14km). Through the gate and immediately **R** through another gate and down the large eroded track down to Nab End Farm (14.7km). **TR** along the road through Oak Tree Farm before climbing back to the carpark (16km).

Shorter Route

When you reach the col below Roseberry Topping (8.6km), **TR** along the Cleveland Way and walk up to the forest corner. Through the gate then bear **L** across Newton Moor and down to the forest. Through the gate then **R** inside the forest edge to the track junction where you rejoin the main route across Hutton Moor.

12. Gisborough Moor

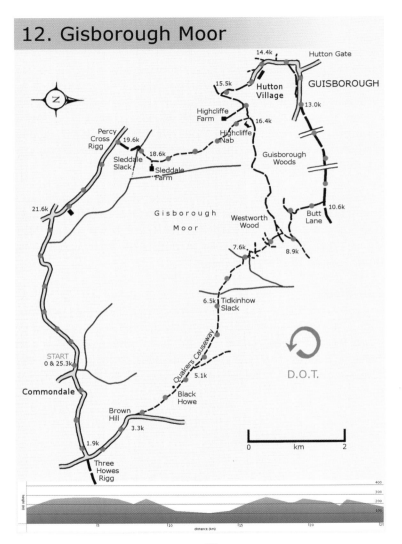

Route Details

Start Grid Ref
GR 663105 Commondale
village

Map
OS26 1:25 000

Distance
Full: 25.3km/15.8m
Short: 20km/12.5m

Height Gain
480m

%age off road
56%

Time
3-4 hours

Facilities
Commondale and
Guisborough

Route Summary

This is an interesting and varied ride, especially for those with a liking for history, as it partly follows one of the ancient pannierman's causeways – paved roads along which pack animals were led – that linked the abbeys of Guisborough and Whitby.

There are also many tumuli on these moors – the remains of Bronze Age graves. There are a variety of tracks including a couple of walking sections but with the compensation of some long descents and some very attractive scenery over Kildale Moor as you head south over Guisborough Moor – which is spelt correctly but differently from Guisborough Abbey.

The Route

Climb the Castleton Road towards Three Howes Rigg (1.9km). **TL** along Brown Hill and when the road swings **R** take the Quakers Causeway bridleway on your **L** (3.3km) across High Moor. This is an old paved track and you reach the flagged section just after passing Black Howes. Bear **L** at the bridleway junction (5.1km) along the single track, passing under some overhead wires after 600m before reaching the fields and following the wall to Tidkinhow Slack (6.5km).

A slight climb then down a lovely single track to Westworth Woods (7.6km). Through the gate then walk up the path to a track, **TL** onto a forest road then **R** to the next junction just inside the forest. Take the path on your **L** through the trees and walk for 300m up to the forest gate (8.2km).

Through the gate into Guisborough Woods and immediately bear **L** along a track then **TR** across a felled area before dropping down to a track. Straight over and down through the trees to a good track where you **TR** (8.6km). Down this wide track then sharp **L** and along to a large junction (9.2km). Bear **R** down to the next junction where you bear **L** for 500m to the next junction. Here turn sharply **R** and follow this track down to the edge of the forest.

Through the gate then down Butt Lane over the bridge before turning **L** (10.6km) and riding parallel to, then joining, the old railway line after 300m. Follow this excellent track through the edge of Guisborough for 2.6km until you reach an old platform. Bear **R** onto the road then immediately **L** at the junction before turning **R** onto the bridleway which takes you back to the road at Hutton Gate. **TL** towards Hutton Village, ignoring 3 bridleways on your **R** and then go straight up forest road (15.2km).

Singletrack trails near Highcliffe Nab, between Guisborough Woods & Gisborough Moor. Rider Graham Hood. Both pics: Dave Johnson

Quaker's Causway. Like titgh rope walking on wheels.

At the top, **TL** and contour for 500m before passing the track to Highcliffe Farm then climbing to the gate below Highcliff Nab (16.4km). **TR** just in front of the gate on a single track to a gate then up the edge of the fields through 2 more gates where you reach Guisborough Moor (17km).

SO for 200m then keep **L** for 300m on a good single track that meets a quad track for 400m before descending to Sleddale Farm (18.6km). **TR** along the farm road, across Sleddale Slack before climbing up to Percy Cross Rigg (19.6km). **TL** and follow the road past Percy Rigg Farm until you reach the crossroads (21.6km). **TL** and a fast descent, tough climb then pleasant ride along the edge of the moors will bring you back to Commondale village (25.3km).

Shorter route

After you have crossed the felled area in Guisborough Woods **TL** along a good track for 200m until you reach the Cleveland Way. Follow this forest road for 2km passing beneath Highcliffe Nab until you reach the forestry gate where you rejoin the main route and **TL** up the grassy bridleway to the fields.

Opp. Commondale White Cross. Always regularly whitewashed as all the Downe Estate boundary stones are – a good rest stop. Pic: Derek Purdy

13. Danby Dale

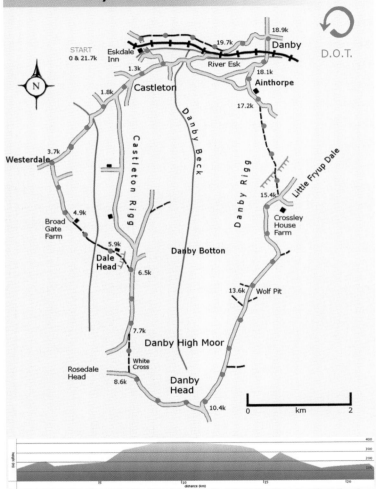

START 0 & 21.7k
Eskdale Inn
1.3k
Castleton
1.8k
River Esk
Danby
18.9k
19.7k
D.O.T.

N

Ainthorpe
18.1k
17.2k

Danby Beck

Castleton Rigg

Westerdale
3.7k

Danby Rigg

Little Fryup Dale

15.4k

Broad Gate Farm
4.9k

5.9k
Dale Head
6.5k

Danby Botton

Crossley House Farm

13.6k   Wolf Pit

7.7k
Danby High Moor

Rosedale Head
White Cross
8.6k

Danby Head

10.4k

km
0   2

Route Details

Start Grid Ref
GR 663105 The Eskdale Inn,
Castleton

Map
OS 26 1:25 000

Distance
Full: 21.7km/14m
Short: 18.5km/11.6m

Height Gain
460m

%age off road
37%

Time
2½ -3 hours

Facilities
Eskdale Inn, Fox and Hounds
at Ainthorpe, Duke of
Wellington at Danby

Route Summary

This is one of the best routes in the book in terms of variety of scenery and shouldn't be too taxing in terms of map reading. There is more road-riding than usual but the views are worth it. You will pass White Cross at the highest point on the ride but it isn't a cross and should really be called 'Fat Betty'.

Legend goes that if ever Betty meets Old Ralph (another cross 500m west) then they will get married. You will also follow the Eskdale valley railway line for the last 4km. Don't forget to visit the Moors Centre at Danby while you are in the area as it contains a wealth of information about the North Yorkshire Moors National Park.

The Route

TR out of the Eskdale Inn carpark, over the River Esk then **L** and up into Castleton village. **TR** up the main street to the road junction at the edge of the moor (1.3km). Go **SO** along the smaller road then down to the road junction in Westerdale (2.2km). **SO** then **L** at the junction just before the village (3.7km).

Follow the road to the end at Broad Gate Farm then straight along the good track, down over the stream and up to Dale Head before the stiff climb (push) onto Casleton Rigg (6.5km). **TR** along the road to the bend where you bear **L** at the bridleway sign (7.7km) and follow this good single track across the moor to White Cross (8.6km).

TL along the road to the next junction at a large unnamed standing stone (10.4km) where you **TL** and eventually head downhill with superb views into the dales on both sides. Pass the Wolf Pit tumulus (13.6km) before dropping into Little Fryup Dale at Crossley House Farm (15.4km). Bear **L** at the road junction up a grassy track until you have to push up to the Danby Rigg skyline (15.9km).

Bear **L** across the moor then down a technical single track through old quarries to a gate (17k). **SO** through gorse bushes to the road then **L** down to Ainthorpe (and the Fox and Hounds). Bear **R** then **TR** through the village before crossing the river and railway line into Danby village.

TL at the crossroads (18.9km), up a short hill and down another before bearing **R** at the bridleway sign (19.7km). Contour along this excellent track across the bottom of the moor, through the woods then past 3 farms before reaching the road where you **TL** down to the Eskdale Inn (21.7km).

Shorter route

When you reach the road junction above Castleton go straight along
the smaller road across the moor but **TL** before this road starts to
drop steeply into Westerdale (1.8km). Follow this road along the
W side of Castleton Rigg, **SO** at the junction above Quarry Farm
(3.3km) then up the hill after Brown Hill House (4.2km) until you
reach the main road.

TL then follow the main route until you reach the Fox and Hounds
at Ainthorpe where you bear **L** and follow the road back into
Castleton.

Danby Lodge, NYM information centre, cafe & carpark. Pic: Derek Purdy

14. Scaling Dam & Danby Beacon

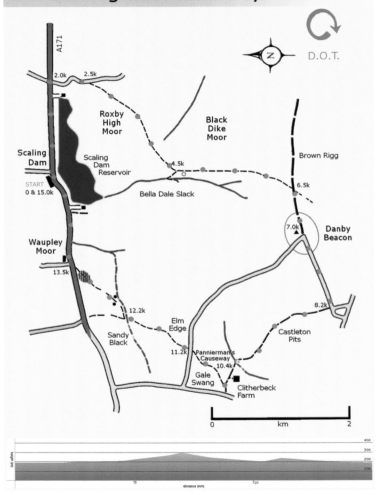

Route 14: Scaling Dam & Danby Beacon

Route Details

Start Grid Ref
GR 742127 The Grapes Inn,
Scaling Dam

Map
O.S27 1:25 000

Distance
Full: 15km/9.5m
Short: 13km/8.1m

Height Gain
120m

%age off road
66%

Time
1½-2 hours

Facilities
Grapes Inn

Route Summary

This is a short demanding
ride from a physical and
navigational point of view.

There are times when there is
no visible track so follow the
directions and keep in contact
with the OS map. Although
heading north to the A171
would be a safe escape option,
it would probably involve
walking.

TL from the carpark along the busy main road towards Whitby beneath the dam of Scaling Reservoir. Pass the carpark then **TR** at the road junction (2km) and follow this minor road for 500m before taking the good singletrack across Roxby High Moor. It improves to a vehicle track after 700m and continues towards the junction at Bella Dale Slack (4.5km). Bear **L** along a singletrack passing a heathery knoll after 200m and continue due **S** across Black Dike Moor gradually climbing to the track junction at Brown Rigg (6.3km). **TR** along the byway to the excellent viewpoint at Danby Beacon (7km). Bear **L** down the road for 1.2km then **TR** at a road junction along a vehicle track towards Castleton Pits.

Contour along this good track with good views of Danby on your **L** until you reach Clitherbeck Farm where you turn sharp **R** just before the road along Pannierman's Causeway (10.4km). Follow this paved singletrack across Gale Swang to the road along Elm Edge (11.2km). Go straight across and gradually down to the wooden bridge over Sandy Slack (12.2km).

Be careful as you bear **R** along the edge of the marsh, where there is no visible track, and up to 2 boundary stones (12.6km) then **SO** towards the pan-tiled roofs in the distance at Waupley Moor; through bracken and then a final push for 200m across some boggy trackless land to the road (13.5km). **TR** and follow the (still) busy road back to Scaling Dam (15km).

[Rte 13]. Danby Rigg. Pic: Steve Willis

Shorter route

When you reach Danby Beacon **TR** along the Elm Edge road for 2.4km until you reach the Pannierman's Causeway where you **TR** and follow the main route.

15. Glaisdale & Fryupdale

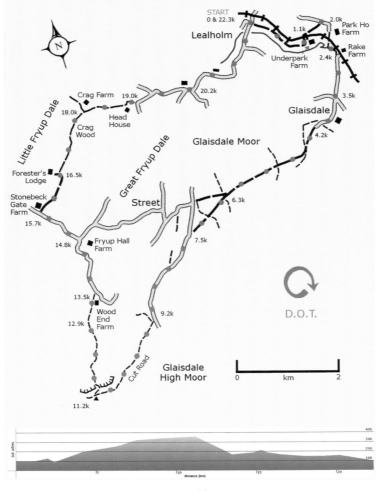

START
0 & 22.3k
Lealholm
2.0k
Park Ho Farm
1.1k
Underpark Farm
2.4k
Rake Farm
3.5k
Glaisdale
4.2k
Crag Farm
19.0k
18.0k
Head House
Crag Wood
Glaisdale Moor
20.2k
Little Fryup Dale
Great Fryup Dale
Forester's Lodge
16.5k
Stonebeck Gate Farm
15.7k
Street
6.3k
14.8k
Fryup Hall Farm
7.5k
13.5k
Wood End Farm
9.2k
12.9k
D.O.T.
Cut Road
Glaisdale High Moor
11.2k
0   km   2

Route 15: Glaisdale & Fryupdale

Route Details

Start Grid Ref
GR 763076 Lealholm village
car park

Map
OS27 1:25,000

Distance
Full: 22.3km/14m
Short: 16km/10m

Height Gain
460m

%age off road
54%

Time
2½ - 3½ hours

Facilities
Board Inn at Lealholm

Route Summary

This route starts in the picturesque village of Lealholm (called Lelum in the Doomsday Book). There is plenty to keep you interested on the early stages as you ride along Eskdale before climbing through Glaisdale onto the moors.

There are superb views towards Whitby (behind you) as you ride along Glaisdale Rigg. The bridleway over the High Moor is quite technical and followed by a short steep descent into the head of Great Fryup Dale. The section in Little Fryup Dale can be muddy so try to pick a dry day.

TL out of the carpark along the bridleway towards Glaisdale until you reach Underpark Farm (1.1km). **TL**, through the railway arch and immediately **R** to a gate then **SO** up a grassy track through the field to another gate and **TR** on the tarmac lane to Park House Farm (2km). Through the gate, down the byway to the ford with a footbridge before pushing up to the road at Rake Farm (2.4km). **SO** up the road to Glaisdale village (3.5km) where you cross the road at The Green. Follow the tarmac road to the moorland gate (4.2km) then contour along the south side of Glaisdale Moor passing a number of bridleways until you reach the road on Glaisdale Rigg (7.5km).

Bear **L** and follow the road for 1.7km until you reach a gate on your **R** that you go through and follow the L-hand bridleway across the heather. You pass a signpost on a ridge (10.2km) and follow the Cut Road to a cairn at the head of Great Fryup Dale (11.2km). **TR** then walk your bike down a steep track before crossing 2 streams and a short climb to a gate.

SO along a good grassy track below the old mine workings to another gate (12.9km) before descending through the fields to Wood End Farm (13.5km). **TL** along the road until you reach the road junction at Fryup Hall Farm where you **TL** then up the hill and down to Stonebeck Gate Farm (15.7km).

TR along a good track towards Forester's Lodge (16.5km) then through the fields to Crag Wood (17.5km). Straight along the bottom of the woods then bear **R** and through a gate just before Crag Farm (18km). Up a pleasant track through the woods then down through a gate (18.5km) and bear **L** after 200m through some holly trees, down to a track and diagonally across before contouring through a field to the road bend below Head House (19km). **TL** and follow the road (and signs) back to Lealholm (22.3km).

Shorter route

When you reach the byway junction on Glaisdale Moor after 6.3km bear **R** and go up to the road. Go straight across and down the road into Great Fryup Dale, bearing **R** after 600m to ride through Street then follow Streets Lane and Nuns Green Lane to the road junction at Fryup Hall Farm. **TR** and follow the rejoin the full route past Stonebeck Gate Farm.

Glaisdale High Moor on the Cut Road. Pic: Phil Hodgkiss

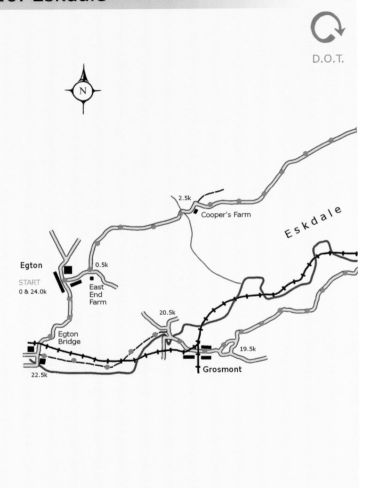

D.O.T.

2.5k

Cooper's Farm

Eskdale

Egton

0.5k

START
0 & 24.0k

East
End
Farm

20.5k

Egton
Bridge

19.5k

22.5k

Grosmont

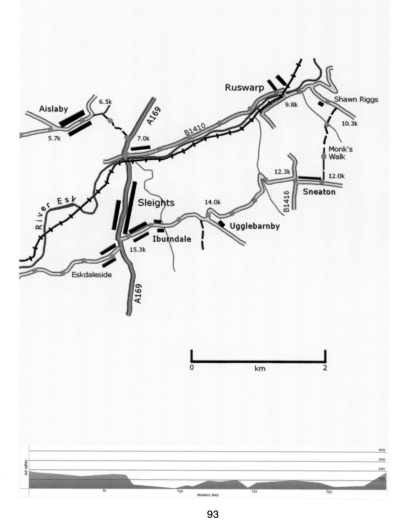

6.5k

A169

Ruswarp

Shawn Riggs

9.8k

10.3k

5.7k

7.0k

B1410

Monk's
Walk

12.3k

12.0k

River Esk

Sleights

14.0k

B1416

Sneaton

Iburndale

Ugglebarnby

15.3k

Eskdaleside

A169

0   km   2

93

Route Details

Start Grid Ref
GR 808066 The Horseshoe
Inn, Egton

Map
O.S27 1:25 000

Distance
Full: 24km/15m
Short: 17km/10.6m

Height Gain
500m

%age off road
16%

Time
2½-3 hours

Facilities
Egton, Aislaby, Sleights,
Ruswarp, Sneaton and
Grosmont

Route Summary

This is the only road route in
the guide with only 3 short
bridleway sections but the
best way to see the beauties
of Eskdale. For much of
the route you will be riding
parallel to the Esk Valley
Railway Line, opened in 1836
mainly to transport ironstone
from the many mines in the
area, and the River Esk that
flows into the North Sea at
Whitby.

There are many picturesque
villages on the route
including Aislaby, Sleights
at the foot of Blue Bank,
Ruswarp where the tidal
stretch of the river ends,
Ugglebarnby, Grosmont
where the 2 railways meet
and Egton where the annual
show has been held for over
100 years.

TL from the carpark then **L** again after 100m signposted Grosmont.
TL at East End Farm (Cycle Route 52) and follow the valley side
that provides fine views of the Eskdale valley. Bear **R** at Coopers
Farm (2.5km) down a short descent then continue to contour to
Aislaby (5.7km). **SO** through the village then, as the road bends **L**
at the speed limit sign, go straight along the vehicle track (6.3km).

[Rte 15] Bouldering on Gaisdale Moor. Pic: Derek Purdy

Follow this for 100m then **TR** down a paved singletrack (which is slippery when wet) to the A169. **TR** down the road then **L** towards Ruswarp for 2.5km. **TR** in the village, over the railway line and river, then **L** at the junction (9.8km).

Follow the River Esk for 300m then up the sharp climb on Shawn Riggs until you reach the bridleway (10.8km). **TR** over the ridge then down to the footbridge and push through the woods before following Monk's Walk to Sneaton (12km).

TR then **R** and **L** over the B1416 towards Ugglebarnby. **TR** down towards Iburndale then climb to the A169 at Sleights. **TL** then **R** towards Grosmont along Eskdaleside and follow this road that climbs and descends frequently crossing several becks until you reach the road junction (19.5km).

TR down the steep descent into Grosmont where you cross the railway line again. **SO** under the railway bridge and out of the village, over the river and bend **R** on the road then **L** along a gravel track on the **N** side of the river (20.5km).

Follow this track for 2km going under the railway again and arriving at Egton Bridge (22.5km). **TR** under another railway bridge then the final steep climb up the road to Egton (24km).

Shorter route

When you reach the Ruswarp junction on the A169 continue along the main road through Sleights up to the edge of the village where you **TR** towards Grosmont.

17. Ravenscar & Robin Hood's Bay

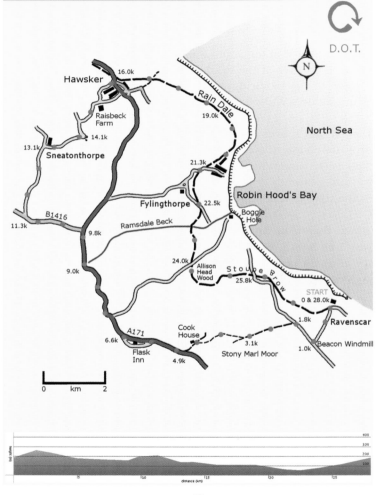

D.O.T.

Hawsker 16.0k

Rain Dale

19.0k

Raisbeck
Farm

North Sea

14.1k

13.1k

Sneatonthorpe

21.3k

Robin Hood's Bay

Fylingthorpe 22.5k

Boggle
Hole

B1416

Ramsdale Beck

11.3k

9.8k

9.0k

24.0k

Allison
Head
Wood

Stoupe Brow

25.8k

START
0 & 28.0k

1.8k

Ravenscar

Cook
House

A171

6.6k

3.1k

1.0k

Beacon Windmill

Flask
Inn

4.9k

Stony Marl Moor

0   km   2

Route 17: Ravenscar & Robin Hood's Bay

Route Details

Start Grid Ref
GR 981017 Car park in Ravenscar

Map
O.S27 1:25 000

Distance
Full: 28.4km/17.7 miles
Short: 21km

Height Gain
350m

%age off road
53%

Time
2½ - 3 hours

Facilities
Flask Inn, Hawsker, Robin Hood's Bay, Ravenscar

Route Summary

This is the only coastal route in the guide and follows the old railway line upgraded to a bridleway for 12km. Ravenscar was built as a tourist attraction to rival Scarborough but it never worked. It is still very spectacular and more famous now as the finish of the Lyke Wake Walk from Osmotherley and the Wainwright Coast to Coast Walk from St Bees Head. After the first moorland section you need to use the busy A171 for 5km so take care. Then, it is quiet country lanes to Hawsker followed by the gentle coastal section to Robin Hoods Bay which has nothing to do with outlaws but is historically famous for its smuggling activities. The last section passes the Peak Alum works on Stoupe Brow which were worked for 2 centuries but have been disused since 1850.

Beginning at the carpark near the Ravenscar Hotel, ride uphill directly away from the sea. Continue **SO** over the old railway line and head for the remains of Beacon Windmill at the road junction (1km). **TR** along Scarborough Road towards the mast on the hill top (1.8km). **TL** and follow the bridleway downhill over Stony Marl Moor bearing **R** when the track divides (3.1km). Contour along a pleasant track before bearing **L** and heading down to Cook House. Bear **L** along the track and follow it to the main road (4.9km).

TR along the busy A171 taking the old road past the Flask Inn after 1km then back onto the main road for another 3km until you reach the B1416 to Ruswarp (9.8km). **TL** for 1.5km then **R** at the first junction along Raikes Lane towards Sneatonthorpe. **TR** at the junction (13.1km) and follow this road crossing 2 streams to Low Hawsker (15.2km). Bear **L** at Raisbeck Farm through the village until the A171. **TL** to the traffic lights, where it is safer to cross the road, then **R** along the excellent old railway line that you follow for the rest of the ride. You're now travelling parallel to the coastline with excellent sea views to your **L** and in front. After 3km you cross Rain Dale reaching Robin Hood's Bay in a further 2km.

Follow the National Cycle Network signs through the village (unless you want to go down to the beach) so that you keep to the old railway line **SW** past Fylingthorpe (21.3km), over Middlewood Lane (22.5km), across Ramsdale Beck, over the Boggle Hole road (24km), through Allison Head Wood before contouring around Stoupe Brow. Cross the Scarborough Road (25.8km) before riding the last 2.5km with more superb views of the finish at Ravenscar (28.4km).

Shorter route

When you reach the A171/B1416 junction (9.8km) continue along the main road for a further 1km before turning **R** across the moor then down to Fylingthorpe and reaching the old railway line on the edge of Robin Hood's Bay. **TR** here and follow the main route back to Ravenscar.

Robin Hood's Bay, definitely worth visiting for the Treasure Island feel. Pic Phil Hodgkiss

18. Littlebeck & Newton House Plantation

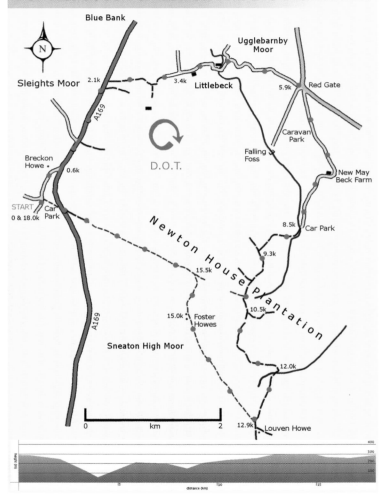

Blue Bank

Uggglebarnby Moor

Sleights Moor

2.1k

3.4k

Littlebeck

5.9k   Red Gate

N

Breckon Howe

0.6k

Caravan Park

Falling Foss

New May Beck Farm

A169

START

0 & 18.0k

Car Park

D.O.T.

8.5k   Car Park

9.3k

Newton House Plantation

15.5k

10.5k

15.0k   Foster Howes

Sneaton High Moor

12.0k

0   km   2

12.9k   Louven Howe

Route 18: Littlebeck & Newton House Plantation

Route Details

Start Grid Ref
GR 852028 Car park at
Breckon Howe Quarries

Map
OS27 1:50 000

Distance
18km/11.2m

Height Gain
350m

%age off road
61%

Time
2 – 2½ hours

Facilities
None

Route Summary

This ride starts and finishes
near the busy A1169 so please
take care. You drop into the
sheltered valley of Littlebeck
before heading for Newton
House Plantation. You can
add an easy extra 3km to
the ride if you want to visit
Falling Foss waterfall.

You reach the moors
at Louven Howe with 2
interesting features separated
by just 4 miles but 1337
years. Lilla Cross is the oldest
Christian cross on the moors
having been erected in AD625
and RAF Fylingdales is a
radar station built in 1962.
The ride then heads along
Foster Howe Rigg that is
better ridden on a dry day.

Head north from the carpark towards Whitby then **L** along the busy A169 to the top of Blue Bank. **TR** through the gate onto the bridleway 100m before the warning sign (2.1km). Follow this good track down the moor passing a pylon then bear **L** at the junction down through a gate and onto tarmac to the road junction (3.4km).

Head straight down into Littlebeck where you bend **L** then **R** at the junction up a very steep road for local traffic only (4.4km). Cross Ugglebarnby Moor to the road junction at Red Gate (5.9km). Take the first road on your **R** if you want to visit Falling Foss but, if not, take the second road on your **R** towards the caravan park which you pass after 500m.

Carry on past the farm before dropping down to the May Beck carpark (8.5km) then up the gravel track for 600m into Newton House Plantation. Through the gate then **L** at the first junction, keep **L** at the second junction then **R** at the third junction after 10.5km. Follow this forestry road for another 2.5km with a slight drop across a stream before climbing onto the moor at Louven Howe (12.9km). **TR** before the main gate and keep on the R-hand side of the fence across Sneaton High Moor.

At Foster Howes tumuli carry **SO** when a track joins from the **L** (15km). After 500m bear left as the forest appears in front of you and the track improves then through another gate after 1km and take care crossing the busy A169 after a further 1km. Follow the track through the heather past the old quarries to the carpark at the Breckon Howe crossroads (18km)

Climbing from Littlebeck Ford; you really won't want to heed the sign's advice. Pic: Phil Hodgkiss

19. Dalby Forest & Fylingdales Moor

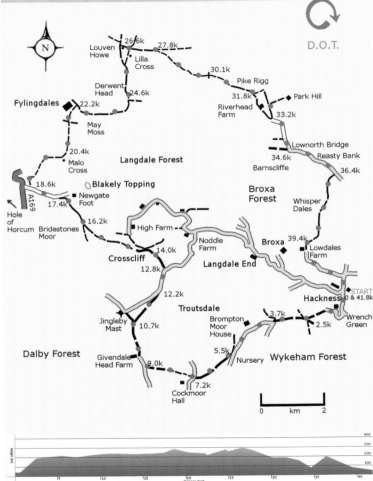

D.O.T.

N

26.6k
27.8k
Louven Howe
Lilla Cross
30.1k
Pike Rigg
Derwent Head
24.6k
31.8k
Park Hill
Fylingdales 22.2k
Riverhead Farm
33.2k
May Moss
Lownorth Bridge
20.4k
34.6k
Reasty Bank
Malo Cross
Langdale Forest
Barnscliffe
36.4k
Blakely Topping
Broxa Forest
18.6k
Newgate Foot
Whisper Dales
A169
17.4k
Hole of Horcum
16.2k
Broxa
39.4k
Bridestones Moor
High Farm
Noddle Farm
Lowdales Farm
14.0k
Crosscliff
Langdale End
12.8k
12.2k
START
Troutsdale
Hackness 0 & 41.8k
Jingleby Mast
10.7k
Brompton Moor House
3.7k
Wrench Green
2.5k
Givendale Head Farm
9.0k
5.5k
Nursery
Wykeham Forest
Dalby Forest
7.2k
Cockmoor Hall
0   km   2

106

Route 19: Dalby Forest & Fylingdale Moor

Route Details

GR 967900 Hackness village
hall

O.S27 1:25 000

Full: 41.8km/26.1 miles
Short: 25km

470m

76%

5 - 6 hours

Everley Arms in Hackness
and Langdale End on shorter
route

Route Summary

This is the longest ride in the
guide. The River Derwent
drains the SE section of the
Moors and is only 4 miles
from the sea at Hackness
but, instead, forced its
way through Forge Valley
during the last ice age before
winding its way for 70 miles
to the Humber Estuary.
Leaving the valley, the route
follows excellent forestry
tracks before reaching
Bridestones Moor.

Saltergate Inn has a fire that
reputedly is never allowed
to go out as the remains of
a murdered excise man are
buried behind. Malo Cross
was erected in 1619 but
disappeared for 50 years
before it was found in a
Pickering garden. You pass
the source of the river at
Derwent Head between RAF
Fylingdales and Lilla Cross
(mentioned in Rte 18) before

riding down the superb Pike Rigg into Harwood Dale. Then it is back up into the forest before a final descent through Whisper Dales.

The Route

TL out of the carpark and head **S** for 600m where you **TR** for Wrench Green. Bear **R**, **R** and **L** up to the edge of Wykeham Forest (1.7km) then up Lang Gate to the forest road junction (2.5km). Bear **R** then **L** along the track to the view point at the road junction (3.7km). **SO** passing the forestry nurseries then bear **R** along a forest track 800m after Brompton Moor House. Continue along the edge of the forest until you reach the earthworks at the head of Troutsdale (7.2km).

Straight across the road along a good track to the tarmac road (9km) where you **TR** passed Givendale Farm into Dalby Forest where you bear **L** along the forest road for 1km. **TR** 400m before Jingleby mast along a good track by the edge of the forest until you meet the forest drive (12.2km). Bear **R** along the tarmac for 600m then bear **L** towards Crosscliff. Do not turn into the carpark but continue until you reach the viewpoint (14km) where you **TL** along an excellent track with superb views to the **N**.

Continue to the edge of the forest (16.2km). Through the gate along the edge of Bridestones Moor until you come to the gate above Newgate Foot (17.4km). **SO** then bear **L** along the tarmac lane to the edge of the wood (18.6km). **TR** through a gate and follow forest edge for 300m then **TR** through a gate into a pasture field. Follow the track curving **L** along the edge of the escarpment above Saltergate Inn. Then through one gate, ignore the diagonal path down to the **L** after a further 300m then down the lovely sloping single track to Malo Cross (20.4km). **TL** through the

Malo Cross, a good waymarker on misty days. Rider John Dixon Pic: Phil Hodgkiss

gate (signposted Lilla Cross) and follow the forest edge on single track across soft ground then heather, and through a gate onto MOD land. Keep close to the forest and across a gravel track, **SO** keeping RAF Fylingdales on your **L** and down to the gate at the fence corner with felled forest on your **R** (22.2km).

TR at the signpost, down and up a concrete track and through the gate. Follow the gravel track keeping the forest on your **R**, bear **L** and pass the main track into Langdale Forest (24.6km) then down to Derwent Head, through a gate and up the gravel track across the moor keeping the fence on your **L**. Ignore the singletrack on your **R** signposted 'Robin Hood's Bay' (25.8km) and continue for another 700m to Louven Howe (26.6km). **TR** along a good track then bear **R** at the next junction (27.8km) before starting the long descent to the gate on the edge of the moor (30.1km). **SO** across the fields then up the track to Pike Rigg (31.8km).

TL through the gate along the field edge for 400m through the gate then **R** along a good track, through a gate and **SO** to the junction **SE** of Riverhead Farm (33.2km). Down this road to Lownorth Bridge (34.6km) then **L** to the junction and bear **R** up Reasty Bank to the carpark (36.4km). **TR** then descend on the forest track into Whisperdales. Follow the track down the valley to Lowdales Farm where you ford 2 streams (39.4km) and continue down the road to Hackness (41.2km) and **TR** to reach the village hall (41.8km).

Shorter route

When you reach the Crosscliff viewpoint (14km) go **SO** down the good track and cross the stream below High Farm. Through the gate then follow the road for 4km to the junction just after Noddle Farm (19km). **SO** down the valley to Langdale End (22km) and follow the road back to Hackness (25km).

James Panton getting airborne in Dalby Forest. Pic: Phil Hodgkiss

20. Newtondale & Dalby Forest

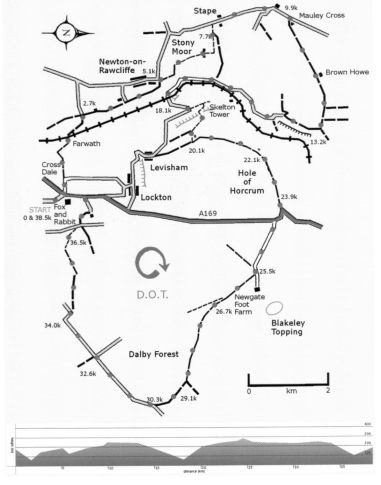

Stape
9.9k
Mauley Cross
7.7k
Stony Moor
Newton-on-Rawcliffe 5.1k
Brown Howe
2.7k
18.1k
Skelton Tower
13.2k
Farwath
20.1k
Cross Dale
Levisham
22.1k
Hole of Horcrum
23.9k
Lockton
A169
START Fox and Rabbit
0 & 38.5k
36.5k
25.5k
D.O.T.
Newgate Foot Farm
26.7k
34.0k
Blakeley Topping
32.6k
Dalby Forest
30.3k 29.1k
0   km   2

Route 20: Newtondale & Dalby Forest

Route Details

Start Grid Ref
GR 845883 Fox and Rabbit
Inn, Pickering to Whitby
Road

Map
O.S27 1:25 000

Distance
Full: 38.5km/24m
Short: 24km/15m

Height Gain
600m

%age off road
70%
Time
4 - 5 hours

Facilities
Fox and Rabbit Inn, Newton on
Rawcliffe, Levisham Station
(plus Levisham and Lockton
villages on the shorter route)

Route Summary

This is a forest and moorland
route either side of the
Newtondale valley. The
valley is famous for the
North Yorkshire Moors
Railway (regularly featured
in 'Heartbeat') that was
originally opened in 1836,
closed in 1965 and reopened
in 1973.

The ride around the rim
of the Hole of Horcum is
especially beautiful when
the heather is in bloom.
Dalby Forest offers a variety
of mountain biking routes
and many other recreational
opportunities.

The Route

Go straight across the busy A169 along a farm road and **SO** at the bend after 400m. Through the gate, across a field then down Cross Dale keeping **R** of the wood then **R** at the bottom and head **N** towards Farwath (1.7km). **TL**, cross the North Yorkshire Moors Railway then climb the vehicle track out of the valley to the crossroads (2.7km). **TR** to Howlgate Farm, along East Brow Road to the farm (by the sewage works) then along the track to Newton on Rawcliffe (5.1km). **TR** next to the road down the good track to Raygate Slack where you bear **L** to the gate (5.9km).

Climb out of the valley then cross Stony Moor on a technical singletrack until you reach Middle Farm (6.7km). **SO** to the field corner then **TL**, follow the field edge until you reach the vehicle track coming out of Seavy Slack and go **SO** to the Stape Road (7.7km). **TR** through Stape, down across the beck then **L** and **R** up to Mauley Cross (9.9km). Bear **R** along the forest road past Brown Howe and Wardle Rigg until you reach the T-junction above Newtondale (13.2km). **TR** and follow this excellent vehicle track for 1km, with superb views of Levisham Moor and the railway line, until you reach the next T-junction. **TL** down the road, round the hairpin bend then **R** at Rapers Farm picnic site (14.7km). Continue down the road with more superb views (of Skelton Tower) down Newtondale until you reach Levisham Station (18.1km). Cross the railway line then climb the steep road until you reach a sharp bend on the moor (18.7km). Head **N** along a grassy bridleway for 400m before turning **R** then bearing **R** and pushing for 300m up a steep slope onto Levisham Moor (19.4km). **TL** towards a wall corner then follow the wall along the edge of the moor until you reach Limpsey Gate (20.1km). Turn sharp **L** down the track to Dundale Pond where you bear **R**, gently climb the moor to Seavy Pond (22.1km) where the track bears **R** around the edge of the Hole of

Horcum to reach the A169 at Saltergate Bank (23.9km). **TR** and follow the bridleway up the Right hand side of the road then cross it carefully at the carpark onto Old Wife's Way (24.3km). Follow this road for 1km downhill (while keeping to the speed limit) and bear **R** just before the road bends **L** (25.5km) and drops down to Newgate Foot. Go through the gate then follow the good track along the edge of Newgate Moor until you reach the forest gate (26.7km). Go through the gate then follow the forest road along the top of Crosscliff Brow passing the viewpoint until you reach the crossroads (29.1km). Bear **R** along the vehicle track until you reach the Dalby Forest Toll Road (30.3km). **TR** along the tarmac to the junction at Jingleby mast (32.6km) where you go **SO** down a tarmac road through the forest. The road bends **R** (34km) then, as it bends **L** after 200m you head diagonally **L** along a vehicle track for 600m until you reach a field corner. Bear **L** and immediately **R** on a forest road following the field edge to the next bend (35.2km). **TR** down a steep path into Seive Dale where you **TL** down the

Dalby Forest's world class built trails. Rider: Mike Mike Hawtin, Pic: Phil Hodgkiss

vehicle track for 800m. Bear **R** along a good singletrack above the fields before descending to the main forest road (36.5km). Go diagonally across and bear **L** down a forest road, crossing Dalby Beck before climbing up out of the valley to Staindale Lodge (37.4km). Bear **L** up the road to the A169 then **L** and back to the Fox and Rabbit (38.5km).

Shorter route

When you reach Levisham Station stay on the road as it climbs all the way into Levisham village. Go straight through the village then down the steep hairpin bend, across the stream and climb into Lockton. Go **SO** at the crossroads then **L** at the junction, bend **R** then **TR** along Hostess Lane to the A169. Bear **R** for 1km back to the carpark (24km).

21. Goathland & Wheeldale

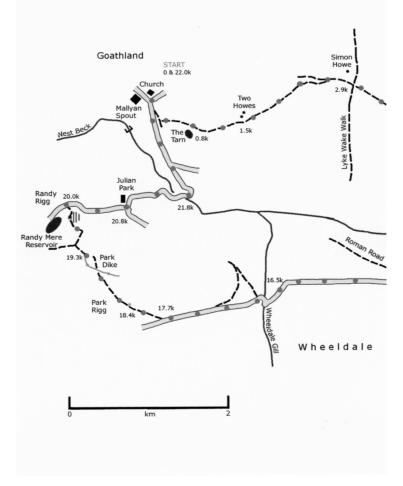

Goathland

Simon Howe

START
0 & 22.0k

2.9k

Church

Two Howes

Mallyan Spout

West Beck

The Tarn 0.8k

1.5k

Lyke Wake Walk

Julian Park

Randy Rigg 20.0k

20.8k

21.8k

Roman Road

Randy Mere Reservoir

19.3k

Park Dike

16.5k

Park Rigg

17.7k

18.4k

Wheeldale Gill

Wheeldale

0   km   2

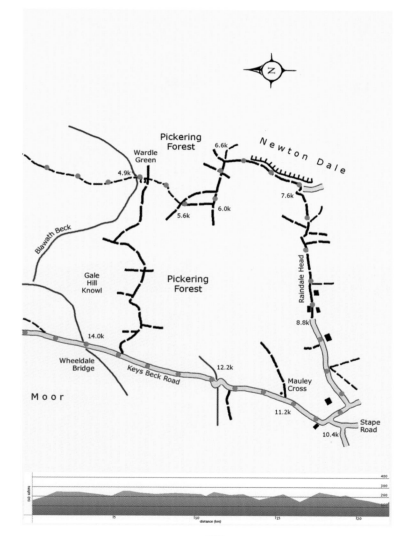

Route Details

Start Grid Ref
GR 827007 Goathland Church

Map
O.S27 1:25 000

Distance
Full: 23km/14.5m
Short: 17km/10.6m

Height Gain
400m

%age off road
48%

Time
2½ - 3½ hours

Start Grid Ref
GR 827007 Goathland Church

Facilities
Goathland

Route Summary

This route starts in Goathland, busier these days due to the popularity of 'Heartbeat' and the North Yorkshire Moors Railway. The first part of the ride past Simon Howe is physically and technically demanding so best ridden on a dry clear day.

The middle section is on the excellent tracks of Pickering Forest before returning to the moors on the old Roman road that is clearly visible near Wheeldale Bridge. Careful navigation is needed across Park Rigg between the Wheeldale road and Randy Rigg before returning to Goathland along the road.

Head **W** away from the church, past the pinfold and immediately bear **L** up the grassy bridlepath at the signpost. **TL** after 200m (100m before the next signpost) and go up the hill past a bench, then over a grassy shoulder to a shallow marshy valley with a pond.

Bear **R** then **L** up the hill to the **L** of The Tarn (0.8k) and follow the eroded singletrack passing marker posts and cairns to the Two Howes tumulus (1.5km). Bear **R** across the moor to a signpost, bear **R** then keep **R** below Simon Howe. Go straight across the Lyke Wake Walk (2.9km) and head straight for the forest on the southern horizon.

Pass a sign post then bear **L**, past a curving wall on your **L** then down and across the stream and up to the gate at Wardle Green (4.9km). Through the gate, past the ruin, up the field along the forest edge. Cross the forest road, up a rough field and through a gate. Bear **R** and pass a 'tired' hawthorn tree, through another gate, bear **L** to the forest corner, through a gate into a better field and diagonally across to another gate (5.6km). Cross the forest road and go **SO** keeping the trees on your **L** and a hedge on your **R** to the forest drive (6km).

TL along the gravel track (cars use this route most weekends so keep on the **L** side of the road), past 2 junctions and **TR** at the T junction (6.6km). Now head along the cliff top for 1km with superb views down into Newtondale and across to Levisham Moor. **TR** at the T junction (7.6km) and follow the forest road to Raindale Head (8.8km). **SO** past 3 farms, bend **R** then down to the Stape road (10.7km).

Bear **R** then up the tarmac road along the forest edge to Mauley Cross (11.2km). **SO** for 1km then down to a ford and up to a gate. **SO** then down to Wheeldale Bridge (14km) and the Roman road. **SO** up a steady climb across the edge of Wheeldale Moor before dropping down to Wheeldale Gill (16.5km). Continue up the road for 1200m to the bridleway sign on your **R**. Head for the single tree (18.4km) on Park Rigg before heading down to the path junction at Park Dike.

Bear **R** then **L** across the heather (heading to the trees in the distance) before dropping down to a field corner (19.3km). Climb up the edge of the field then **TR** through a gate before crossing the field for 150m to another gate then down a good track in trees to the marsh outside the wall at Randymere Reservoir. Follow the wall up to the road on Randy Rigg (20km). **TR** and follow the road past Julian Park, down across West Beck then up, **L** and back to Goathland (23km).

Shorter route

When you reach the forest road at Wardle Rigg (6km), **TR** and follow the forest roads across Gale Hill Knoll. **TR** when you reach Keys Beck Road and follow the full route towards Wheeldale Bridge.

22. Cropton Forest & Rosedale

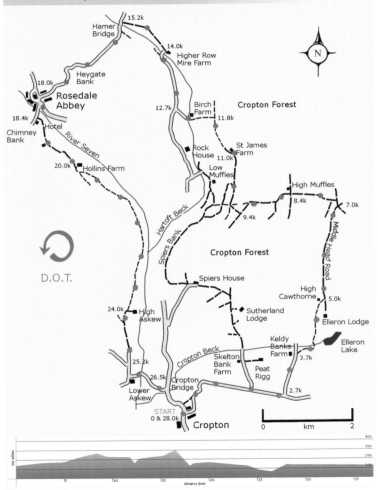

Route Details

Start Grid Ref
GR 755889 The New Inn,
Cropton village

Map
O.S26 & 27 1:25 000

Distance
Full: 27.5km/17.2m
Short: 23km/14.4m

Height Gain
470m

%age off road
62%

Time
3 - 4 hours

Facilities
New Inn and Rosedale Abbey

Route Summary

This ride starts in Cropton village before dropping into Cropton Forest. After crossing Hartoft Beck twice you will climb onto the moors at Hamer Bridge before dropping into Rosedale Abbey where there is more evidence of the iron ore industry than the Cistercian priory.

A short climb up the start of Chimney Bank leads to a lovely bridleway that follows the western side of the River Seven to Cropton Bridge.

TL out of the New Inn carpark, then **R** at Cropton village green. Follow the road **NE** then **E** to the sign to Keldy Cabins (2.7km). **TL** down the hill to Keldy Bank Farm and **TR** along the bridleway just inside the wood (3.7km). Follow the singletrack to the stream and bend **L** up the hill and along a lovely track through the woods passing Elleron Lodge on your R.

Through the gate across a field then **R** and **L** at High Cawthorne (5km). Along Middle Head Road (track) until you reach the forest road junction NW of Stape (7km). Bear **L** then **L** after 100m along the forest road to High Muffles (8.4km). **L** then **R** along the forest road then bear **R** at the next junction heading **W** then **SW** to the next junction (9.4km).

TR then **R** again after 300m and contour for 500m. **SO** at the next junction before heading downhill to the forest gate at St James Farm (11km). **SO**, through another gate along a good track on the edge of the forest to the bridleway junction (11.8km). **TL** through the gate, down the grassy track to Birch Farm where you cross Hartoft Beck then up the tarmac lane to the road junction (12.7km).

TR for 1300m before dropping down over the beck again and up to High Row Mires Farm. **TL** along a farm track through the fields then across the moor to the road at Hamer Bridge (15.2km). **TL** up the road then down Heygate Bank into Rosedale Abbey (18km).

TL then **R** up Chimney Bank road to the White Horse Hotel (18.4km). **TL** and follow this farm track until you reach Hollins Farm (20km). **TR** and push up the grassy bridleway for 100m then bear **L** at the junction and follow the single/quad track for 4km to